W9-DHM-460

DeMOLISHING

SUPPOSED BIBLE

CONTRADICTIONS

EXPLORING FORTY ALLEGED CONTRADICTIONS

First printing: October 2010

Copyright © 2010 by Answers in Genesis–USA. All rights reserved.
No part of this book may be used or reproduced in any manner
whatsoever without written permission of the publisher, except in
the case of brief quotations in articles and reviews. For information
write:

Master Books®, P.O. Box 726, Green Forest, AR 72638

Master Books® is a division of the New Leaf Publishing Group, Inc.

ISBN: 978-0-89051-600-3
Library of Congress Number: 2010937902

Unless otherwise noted, Scripture quotations are from the New
King James Version of the Bible.

Please consider requesting that a copy of this volume be purchased
by your local library system.

Printed in the United States of America

Please visit our website for other great titles:
www.masterbooks.net

For information regarding author interviews,
please contact the publicity department at (870) 438-5288

Master
Books®
A Division of New Leaf Publishing Group

Acknowledgments

We would like to say thanks to all the reviewers of the various chapters in this book. They are: Steve Fazekas, Dr. Terry Mortenson, Frost Smith, Peter Galling, Bodie Hodge, Roger Patterson, Paul F. Taylor, Stacia McKeever, Gary Vaterlaus, Dr. Jason Lisle, Dr. Georgia Purdom, John Upchurch, Ken Ham, and Dr. Tommy Mitchell.

Contents

Each contradiction could often be listed in multiple places, so we merely selected one of the relevant verses and put it under that section.

Acts – Revelation

Foreword

O Timothy! Guard what was committed to your trust, avoiding the profane and idle babblings and contradictions of what is falsely called knowledge — by professing it some have strayed concerning the faith. Grace be with you. Amen (1 Timothy 6:20–21).

In more than 30 years of defending the authority of the Bible from its very first verse, I can't recall the number of times that someone has told me there are contradictions in the Bible. I ask them to name one. This is usually followed by silence, or perhaps a few vain attempts to name one.

Many people today buy into the assertion that the Bible is "full of contradictions," but they haven't bothered to look into the claim for themselves. Since God's Word is perfect, any alleged contradiction in the Bible is going to be due to fallible, imperfect people having misconceptions. I have found time and time again that when an alleged Bible contradiction is brought up, it only takes a little research to refute it.

Most Christians, however, fail to give a good answer when they are presented with an alleged contradiction. This is especially true regarding the Book of Genesis and the charge that evolution/millions of years contradicts the Bible. The inability to have answers to such claims has had a particular effect on the youth in our churches. In my co-authored book *Already Gone,* which presents statistics about young adults (in their 20s) who have walked away from their conservative churches, 44 percent said they did not view the Bible as true and accurate. These 44 percent were asked "why?" Some of the top responses were:

24 percent — the Bible was written by men (which means the Bible would be in contradiction, for it calls itself the Word of God)

15 percent — the Bible contradicts itself

14 percent — science shows the world is old (which signifies that the Bible in Genesis is in contradiction)

11 percent — the Bible has errors (which means again that it is in contradiction)

4 percent — evolution proves the Bible is wrong (another alleged Bible contradiction)[1]

At least 68 percent of these young adults gave an answer that indicated that the Bible had contradictions. It should make you wonder: would they have walked away from the faith if they had answers for these many alleged contradictions when growing up?

These sad statistics show why it is so important for Christians to answer the alleged Bible contradictions. These young people would have discovered how easy it is to answer the challenges. This book is a great starting point in answering these alleged difficulties, and to teach you *how to think* and then *respond* to such claims. Otherwise, just as the Apostle Paul said to Timothy, they could stray from the faith. When Paul wrote these words about 2,000 years ago, he was warning Timothy to avoid a number of things, including *contradictions* that lead to false knowledge. We should heed this advice as well, and not buy into false claims, as some Christians have (including many seminary and Bible college professors). When even some professing Christians bring up alleged contradictions in Scripture, they have a contradiction of their own to tackle: how can they call the Bible the Word of God and say God got some things wrong?

I hope this book will be an encouragement as it equips you to stand on the authority of God's Word with all boldness and without compromise.

— Ken Ham
President and CEO,
Answers in Genesis

---

1. Ken Ham and Britt Beemer, *Already Gone* (Green Forest, AR: Master Books, 2009), p. 107.

Introduction

Dr. Jason Lisle

"You can't trust the Bible! It's full of contradictions!"

It is a popular view these days. Many people have the impression that the Bible is simply an outdated book of fairy tales and contradictions. We are told that biblical stories are fine for children, and perhaps they even contain some moral value. "But surely" says the critic, "such stories cannot be taken seriously in our modern age of science and technology."

After all, the Bible speaks of floating ax-heads, the sun apparently going backward, a universe created in six days, an earth that has pillars and corners, people walking on water, light before the sun, a talking snake, a talking donkey, dragons, and a senior citizen taking two of every animal on a big boat! On the surface, these things may seem absurd, particularly to those unfamiliar with the Christian worldview. But to make matters even worse, it is alleged that the Bible contains *contradictions*. That is, the Bible seems to say one thing in one place, and then the opposite in another. Which are we to believe? Obviously, two contradictory statements cannot both be true.

While we might come to accept many of the peculiar claims of Scripture, a genuine contradiction cannot be true *even in principle*. It is not possible to have a sunny night, a married bachelor, dry water, a true falsehood, and so on. Thus, the claim that the Bible contains contradictions is a serious challenge indeed. For if the Bible has even one real contradiction, then it cannot be completely true. Yet the Christian asserts that the Bible is the Word of God and without error. The claim of contradictions is a serious allegation against the Christian worldview, and we must be prepared to defend the Bible against such claims.

Logical vs. Psychological Problems

Aside from the claim of contradictions, most objections to the Bible are not actually problems at all from a logical perspective. For example, suppose that someone claims, "The Bible can't be trusted because it contains accounts of miracles, and miracles are clearly impossible." This argument is not rationally sound because it *begs the question*. Clearly, an all-powerful God as described in the Bible would be capable of doing miracles. Thus, by merely assuming that miracles are impossible, the critic has already dismissed the possibility that the Bible is true. His argument is circular. The critic is essentially arguing that the Bible is false because the Bible is false.

But if the Bible is true, then certainly it is not a problem for an all-powerful God to make the sun go backward, to walk on water, to make a donkey talk, or to raise the dead. These things may seem counter-intuitive, but they are not *illogical*. They are merely a *psychological* problem for some. Someone may subjectively feel that it is impossible for the sun to go backward as suggested in 2 Kings 20:11, but there is nothing illogical about an all-powerful God doing just that. To argue that something is impossible because it "seems" counter-intuitive is not rational. Just imagine a lawyer arguing that his client is innocent by saying, "Your Honor, I just really, really believe in my heart that he is innocent. I just don't feel that he could have done it." This is nothing more than a mere opinion; it is not evidence at all and would be a silly argument.

Yet people apply this same kind of thinking to the Bible. They essentially argue that the Bible cannot be true because it doesn't "feel" right to them. Whenever someone asserts that miracles are impossible or that some biblical claim doesn't "seem" plausible, he is essentially just assuming that the Bible is false. These kinds of assertions need no refutation because they are not *logical* objections, merely psychological opinions. They simply tell us about the emotional state of the critic rather than presenting a genuine challenge to the Christian worldview.

The Challenge of Contradictions

But contradictions are different. If the Bible asserts a particular claim and also asserts a contrary claim, clearly they cannot both be true at the same time. If the Bible contains genuinely contradictory information, then it cannot really be completely true, since one of the two claims would have to be false. Thus, unlike mere subjective opinions about what is plausible, the claim that the Bible contains contradictions is a real challenge — one that Christians should take seriously.

But what constitutes a contradiction? Most alleged biblical contradictions are not even "apparent" contradictions because there is no necessary conflict between the two propositions. For example, the statements, "Jesus is descended from Adam" and "Jesus is descended from Noah" are not contradictory since both are true. A contradiction is a proposition and its negation (symbolically written, "A and not A") at the same time and in the same relationship. The law of non-contradiction states that a contradiction cannot be true: "It is impossible to have A and not A at the same time and in the same relationship." The last part of this definition is crucially important. Obviously, A and not A could each be true at *different* times. And this resolves a number of alleged biblical contradictions. They could even be true at the same time if the relationship is different.

Difference of Sense or Relationship

Since words can be used in different senses, it is possible to have A and not A at the same time as long as the relationship or sense of the word is different. A man can be a bachelor and also married, in the sense that he is "married to his job." This does not conflict with the fact that the bachelor is unmarried in the sense of not having a wife. There is no contradiction if the sense of the word differs. Some of the alleged Bible contradictions fall under this category. For example, it is claimed that James contradicts Romans on the topic of justification.

Demolishing Contradictions

Romans 4:2–3 teaches that Abraham was justified by faith alone, not by works. However, James 2:21, 24 teaches that Abraham was justified by works and not by faith alone. Do we have a contradiction here? We do have A and not A at the same time, but the relationship differs. Romans 4 is teaching about justification before God; by faith alone, Abraham was considered righteous *before God*. But James 2 is teaching about justification *before men* (James 2:18); by works (as a result of faith), Abraham was considered righteous before men. There is no contradiction here.

Along the same lines, the Trinity is sometimes alleged to be a contradictory concept: "How can God be both one and three?" But upon inspection, we can see that there is no contradiction because the relationship differs. The Bible teaches that God is one in one sense, and three in a *different* sense. Specifically, there is one God (Isaiah 45:5–6, 18, 22), and yet there are three persons who are God: the Father (Galatians 1:1), the Son (John 20:31), and the Holy Spirit (Acts 5:3–4). It may seem counterintuitive that God is one in nature and three in persons, but there is no *contradiction* here. The Trinity may be a psychological problem for some people, but it is not a logical problem.

False Dilemma

Some alleged contradictions of the Bible are presented as a dilemma: "Was the Bible given by inspiration of God as indicated in 2 Timothy 3:16, or was it written by men as indicated in other passages (Luke 1:3; John 21:24)?" The implication is that only one of these can be true, and so, the Bible must contain errors. But this is the *fallacy of the false dilemma* because there is no reason why the Bible cannot be both inspired by God and also written by men. God used men to write His Word (2 Peter 1:21). Another example of a false dilemma is when two words or names are synonymous: Is Reuben the son of Jacob (Genesis 35:22–23) or the son of Israel (Genesis 46:8)? Both are true because Israel is Jacob.

Contextual Considerations

Some examples of alleged contradictions commit the fallacy of *taking the text out of context*. For example, Genesis 1:1 indicates that God exists and has made everything. Suppose someone argued that this contradicts Psalm 14:1, in which we read "there is no God." But to suppose that this is a contradiction would be absurd, since the excerpt from the Psalms is out of context. In context, Psalm 14:1 teaches that "The fool has said in his heart, 'There is no God.' " When the context is considered, there is no contradiction at all. We must remember that the Bible records statements and events that it does not endorse.

Clearly, we must endeavor to honor the author's intentions whenever we study any work of literature. The Bible is no exception. Historical narrations should be taken in the normal (literal) way. Poetic passages in the Bible should not be pressed beyond their intention. Prophetic sections that use a lot of verbal imagery should be taken as such. Figures of speech in the Bible should not be taken as anything other than figures of speech. No, the earth does not *literally* have pillars, or corners, but it does *figuratively*. Even today a person may be considered a "pillar of the community," and we still sometimes use the "four corners of the earth" as a reference to the cardinal directions. To suggest that such passages are teaching a flat earth is unwarranted, and commits the fallacy of taking the text out of context.

There are places where the Bible uses language of appearance, where something is described as it appears from a human perspective. Obvious examples are where the Bible mentions sunrise and sunset. When we examine the context of such verses, it is clear that the authors are not advancing an astronomical model; they are talking about sunrise and sunset (or the direction thereof: east and west, respectively) in the same sense that we do today. It would be fallacious to pull such verses out of context to argue that the Bible is teaching that the sun goes around the earth in a Newtonian physics sense.

Demolishing Contradictions

Fallacy of Sweeping Generalization

There are a number of places where the Bible speaks in terms of generalizations — things that are usually (but not universally) true. The Book of Proverbs contains many of these. It is not a contradiction to have some instances where the general rule does not apply. Therefore, we must be careful not to commit the fallacy of a *sweeping generalization* — applying a general principle as if it were a universal rule. The Proverbs are not intended to be taken as universal rules, but rather as general principles that work most of the time.

Moreover, the Bible also contains things that are indeed rules, but that have acceptable exemptions. Clearly, the Bible teaches that it is wrong to kill, and yet understandably makes exceptions for self-defense, punishment for certain extreme crimes, and during battle. Exceptions to a general principle or exemptions to a rule are not contradictions and thus pose no challenge to the Christian worldview.

Translational Issues

Another difficulty arises due to the fact that most of us read the Bible in a different language than the original. This allows for the possibility of translational issues. One example of confusion that can arise due to translation is found in John 21:15–17. Here Jesus asks Peter three times, "Do you love me?" Peter replies three times that he does love Jesus. In English translations, one word is used for love in all instances, and so, the conversation seems strange. However, in Greek, two words for love are used. When Jesus asks if Peter loves Him, He uses the word agape — intending a selfless, godly love. However, when Peter answers he uses the word phileo — intending brotherly love. Although love is a perfectly correct way to translate both of these words, some of the subtlety of the original is lost in English versions.

In some instances the correct English translation of a word is disputed. In such cases, it is often helpful to consult several different versions of the Bible to see the range of possible interpretations, or to consult a Hebrew/Greek lexicon. Recall that we should always attempt to honor the intentions of the author, and in many cases this entails a careful study of the word or phrase in question. It would be disingenuous to accuse the Bible of a contradiction in an English translation when there is no contradiction in the original language.

Additionally, there are very slight variations in ancient manuscripts of the Bible. Although none of the ancient variants differ in any essential way, some do contain differences of numbers, spelling, and an occasional word or phrase. In most cases, it is easy to tell from context which variant is the original. Variations in ancient manuscripts that are clearly copyist errors should not be taken as the intention of the author, since the author is not responsible for transmission errors. The consistent Christian does not claim that a miscopying of Scripture contains no errors — only that the original manuscripts contained none, since they were divinely inspired. Therefore, an alleged contradiction can be dismissed if the ancient manuscripts do not contain the error.

Contradictions of Inference

Nor are *contradictions of inference* a genuine problem for the Christian worldview. A contradiction of inference is where we merely *infer* a contradiction that the text does not actually state. As one example, we might ask, "Where did Mary and Joseph take Jesus after Bethlehem?" Matthew 2:13–15 indicates that they went to Egypt to be safe from King Herod. However, Luke 2:22, 39 indicates that they took the child to Jerusalem (only a few miles from Bethlehem) and then to Nazareth after that. There is no mention of Egypt in Luke's account. Is this a contradiction?

Although we might *infer* that both Matthew and Luke are describing the same time period and the same visit to the Bethlehem region, the text does not actually state this. Perhaps Matthew is describing a second journey to Bethlehem (or possibly one of the surrounding regions); in fact, the visit of the wise men may have been as much as two years after the birth of Christ, according to Matthew 2:16. So it may be that Joseph and his family went to Nazareth a few months after the birth of Christ in Bethlehem and then to Egypt after their second trip to the Bethlehem region. Although this is only one possibility, the point is that there is no necessary contradiction between Matthew 2 and Luke 2. Any apparent conflict exists only in the mind, not in the text.

Another contradiction of inference is what we might call the *X and only X fallacy*. This occurs when a reader erroneously assumes that a number stated in the Bible (X) indicates *only X* and not more. As an example, consider the account of the demon-possessed man recorded in Mark 5:2–16 and Luke 8:26–37. According to Matthew 8:28–34, there were two men who were demon-possessed. Does this conflict with Mark and Luke? We might be inclined to *infer* from Mark and Luke that there was *only* one man, but the text does not actually say this.

So to call this a contradiction is to commit the X and only X fallacy. After all, if there were two men, then it must also be true that there was one man (as well as one other man)! The fact that Mark and Luke do not mention the other man is interesting. Perhaps one man was much more violent or otherwise noteworthy than the other; we can only speculate. In any case, Mark and Luke do not say that there was *only* one man; therefore, there is no contradiction here.

Contradictions of inference tell us that we have incorrectly imagined the details that were not provided by the text. They are not problems with the Bible because such contradictions exist only in our speculations, not in the biblical text. We must always be careful about drawing dogmatic conclusions from things the Bible does not actually state.

Factual Contradictions and Begging the Question

Another type of criticism might be called an *apparent factual contradiction*. In this case, rather than claiming that the Bible contradicts itself, the critic alleges that the Bible contradicts a well-established fact. There are two types of alleged factual contradictions, and both turn out to be fallacious. The first type comes from a misreading of the text. This could stem from any of the fallacies already listed. A word could be taken in the wrong sense; a verse could be taken out of context; there could be a translational or manuscript dispute; or something could be assumed to be a teaching of Scripture when in fact it is only an inference by the reader.

An example of this type of alleged factual contradiction is the claim that the Bible teaches that the earth is stationary, which contradicts the fact that the earth moves around the sun. In this case, the biblical passages (such as Psalm 93:1, 96:10) have been taken out of context. These are poetic passages indicating the world has been established by God and will not deviate from His plan. These poems are not attempting to develop an astronomical model, and say nothing about physical motion. In fact, the Psalmist also says, "I shall not be moved" (Psalm 16:8; KJV). Clearly, the author does not intend that he will be physically stationary — rather he means that he will not deviate from the path God has created for him.

In the second kind of alleged factual contradiction, the critic has understood the biblical text properly, but is confused about what the external facts actually are. In this case, secular beliefs are assumed to be facts that are beyond question. Examples include: the big bang, evolution, a billions-of-years' time scale, naturalism, and the secular order of events. The Bible does indeed contradict all of these things, but the critic merely assumes that it is the Bible that is wrong. He then argues that since the Bible contradicts these "facts," it must be wrong. But this is the fallacy of *begging the question*. The critic has simply assumed that the Bible is wrong (by assuming the secular claims are true), and then uses this to argue that the Bible is wrong. This is nothing more than a vicious circular argument.

The Law of Non-Contradiction — a Problem for the Non-Christian

The critic asserts that the Bible is false because it contains contradictions. Perhaps the most intriguing aspect of this claim is that it actually backfires on the critic. The reason is this: *only if the Bible is true would contradictions be unacceptable*! Most people simply assume the law of non-contradiction; they take it for granted that a contradiction cannot be true. But have you ever stopped to think about why a contradiction cannot be true?

According to the Bible, all truth is in God (Colossians 2:3; Proverbs 1:7), and God cannot deny (go against) Himself (2 Timothy 2:13). So it makes sense that truth cannot go against itself. Since the sovereign, eternal God is constantly upholding the entire universe by His power (Hebrews 1:3), the Christian expects that no contradiction could possibly happen anywhere in the universe at any time. The universal, unchanging law of non-contradiction stems from God's self-consistent nature.

But apart from the Bible, how could we know that contradictions are *always* false? We could only say that they have been false in our experience. But our experiences are very limited, and no one has experienced the future. So if someone claimed that he or she has finally discovered a true contradiction, the non-Christian has no basis for dismissing such a claim. Only in a biblical worldview can we know that contradictions are always false; only the Christian has a basis for the *law* of non-contradiction.

The Bible tells us that all knowledge comes from God (Colossians 2:3), and when we reject biblical principles, we are reduced to foolishness (Proverbs 1:7). We see this demonstrated in the critic who tries to use God's laws of logic to disprove the Bible. Such an attempt can only fail. The law of non-contradiction is a *biblical principle*. Therefore, whenever anyone uses that law as a basis for what is possible, he or she is tacitly assuming that the Bible is true. The critic of the Bible must use biblical principles in order to argue against the Bible. In order for his argument to be meaningful, it would have to be wrong.

Summary and Conclusions

In this introduction, we've seen that many criticisms of the Bible are not even alleged contradictions, but mere opinions about what is possible. These are not logical problems for the Bible; they are simply psychological problems for the critic. A contradiction would be "A and not A at the same time and in the same relationship." Many alleged biblical contradictions have been asserted. But in most cases we find that A and not A are *not* at the same time, or are used in a *different* sense or relationship and are thus not contradictions at all. The critic sometimes presents a pair of biblical principles as if they were two mutually exclusive options, when, in fact, this is not the case — a *false dilemma.*

In other instances, we find that the words or phrases have been taken *out of context*: poetic passages taken hyper-literally, figures of speech not taken as such, or language of appearance taken as a Newtonian physics. Sometimes critics commit the fallacy of *sweeping generalization*: taking a general principle as if it were universally true, or taking a rule as if it had no exceptions. Some alleged contradictions are nothing more than a *translational or manuscript issue*; the original text contains no contradiction at all.

Additionally, a number of contradictions are merely erroneous *inferences*: they exist only in the mind of the critic, not in the biblical text. One in particular that occurs frequently is when the critic assumes that a number (X) means "only X" when the Bible does not state this. Also, the Bible is sometimes alleged to conflict with an external "fact." A number of these claims stem from a misreading of Scripture. In other cases, the critic has simply assumed that the Bible is in error when it contradicts a particular belief. In doing so, the critic has committed the fallacy of *begging the question.*

Perhaps most significantly, we have shown that any claim of alleged contradiction actually *confirms* that the Bible is true. This is because the law of non-contradiction is based on the biblical worldview. When the critic accepts that a contradiction cannot possibly be true, he has implicitly presumed that the Bible must be true.

So when someone alleges that the Bible cannot be trusted because it contains contradictions, we might turn the question around and simply ask him, "If the Bible is not true, then why would contradictions be *wrong*?" If the Bible were not true, there would be no basis for saying that contradictions are always false; thus, the critic could not argue that the Bible must be false for allegedly containing them. But if the Bible is true, then it cannot have contradictions. Thus, alleged contradictions really cannot possibly be a problem for the Bible — even in principle.

Nonetheless, it is appropriate to be aware of some of the most frequently cited claims of contradictions and to understand the details of why such claims fail when we understand the context. This will serve to confirm that the Bible does not contain contradictions; it is true in its entirety. Alleged contradictions turn out to be nothing more than fallacious reasoning of the critic. Essentially, all of the claims addressed in this book fall under one of the categories listed above; but it is helpful to see each one fleshed-out, lest we be accused of skirting the hard questions.

The Bible tells us "but sanctify Christ as Lord in your hearts, always being ready to make a defense to everyone who asks you to give an account for the hope that is in you, yet with gentleness and reverence" (1 Peter 3:15; NASB). In this spirit, we offer this book. We trust it will affirm the faith of Christians and challenge the beliefs of non-Christians. We pray this series will glorify our Lord Jesus, "in whom are hidden all the treasures of wisdom and knowledge" (Colossians 2:3; NASB).

Genesis

Meat of the Matter

Bodie Hodge

Was Abel eating meat soon after the Curse when he wasn't supposed to be (Genesis 1:29), since he kept the flocks and sacrificed an animal in Genesis 4:2–4?

This alleged contradiction comes from assuming Abel was doing something that Scripture doesn't say he was. The relevant passages are:

> And God said, "See, I have given you every herb that yields seed which is on the face of all the earth, and every tree whose fruit yields seed; to you it shall be for food" (Genesis 1:29).

> Then she bore again, this time his brother Abel. Now Abel was a keeper of sheep, but Cain was a tiller of the ground. And in the process of time it came to pass that Cain brought an offering of the fruit of the ground to the LORD. Abel also brought of the firstborn of his flock and of their fat. And the LORD respected Abel and his offering (Genesis 4:2–4).

Those assuming this is a contradiction are assuming that Abel, who was commanded by God to be vegetarian, was eating the meat from his sacrifice. Matthew indicates that Abel was righteous and therefore was surely not being disobedient to God's command in Genesis 1:29 to be vegetarian.[2]

> So that upon you may fall the guilt of all the righteous blood shed on earth, from the blood of righteous Abel to the blood of Zechariah, the son of Berechiah, whom you murdered between the temple and the altar (Matthew 23:35; NASB).

So, there is no reason to assume that Abel was eating any of the meat — and thus, there is no contradiction.

---

2. It wasn't until Genesis 9:3 that mankind was permitted to eat meat.

As an aside, then, why was Abel tending the flocks? We need to consider that flocks can yield many other things, such as wool, milk, leather, sacrifices for sin, etc.

A fattened (well-fed and tended) lamb, for example, would likely be the one that would be producing the most wool, had the most life ahead of it, and so on; hence the most valuable. So when Abel sacrificed the fattened ones, he was offering his best, and it was a blood sacrifice. This sacrifice was acceptable to the Lord, as it mimicked what God did with Adam and Eve as blood sacrifice (Genesis 3:21) to cover their sins (Hebrews 9:22).

The passage doesn't indicate that Abel *ate* of the sacrifice, so there is really no reason to assume he did. When God sacrificed animals to cover Adam and Eve's sin, there is no indication that they ate either, and since Abel mimicked what God did, then there is no reason to believe that he would have eaten from the sacrifice.

The first possibility of eating the sacrifice would have been with Noah and his family after the Flood when they sacrificed and God told them they were not restricted to vegetarian meals (Genesis 8:20–9:3), although some of those who perished in the Flood may have disobeyed and eaten meat earlier.

Time of Death

Bodie Hodge

Why didn't Adam and Eve die the moment they ate, as Genesis 2:17 implies?

The basis for this questions stems from Genesis 2:17, where Adam was told not to eat from forbidden fruit.

> ". . . but of the tree of the knowledge of good and evil you shall not eat, for in the day that you eat of it you shall surely die" (Genesis 2:17).

Some have claimed that the Bible doesn't necessarily mean what it says in Genesis 2:17 since Adam and Eve didn't die the moment they ate. They argue that the passage really means "die," not "surely die," which is what gives the implication that Adam and Eve should have died that day.[3]

Die That Day or Begin to Die?

It is true that Adam and Eve didn't die the exact day they ate the fruit (Genesis 5:4–5), as some seem to think Genesis 2:17 implies. So, the options are either that God was in error or man's interpretation is in error. But God cannot lie (Hebrews 6:18), so then fallible humans must be making the mistake. Let's take a look at where the confusion begins to arise. The Hebrew phrase in English is more literally:

> "Tree knowledge good evil eat day eat die (dying) die."

The Hebrew is "die die" (*muwth—muwth*) with two different verb tenses (dying and die), which can be translated as "surely die" or literally as "dying you shall die," indicating the beginning of

---

3. For a more technical discussion of this topic, see: Genesis 2:17 — "you shall surely die," Dr. Terry Mortenson, Answers in Genesis website, May 2, 2007: http://www.answersin-genesis.org/articles/2007/05/02/dying-you-shall-die.

dying — an ingressive sense — and finally culminating with death. At the point when they ate, Adam and Eve began to die and would return to dust (Genesis 3:19). If they were meant to die right then, God would have used *muwth* only once, as is used in the Hebrew to mean dead, died, or die, not beginning to die or surely die as die-die is used in Hebrew. Old Testament authors understood this and used the terms appropriately, but sometimes we lose a little during translation.

There are primarily two ways people translate: one is literal or word-for-word, and the other is dynamic equivalence or thought-for-thought. If this were translated word-for-word, it would be "dying die" or "die die," which is difficult for English readers to understand since our grammatical construct doesn't have a changed emphasis when a word is repeated. The *Latin Vulgate* by Jerome, which permits such grammatical constructs, does translate this as "dying die" or "dying you will die" *(morte morieris)*. So most translations into English rightly use a more dynamic equivalence and say "surely die," which implies that it isn't an instant death but will certainly happen (surely).

What Is *Yom* Referring To?

With regard to the Hebrew word *yom* for "day" in Genesis 2:17, it refers directly to the following action — eating — not the latter "dying die." For example, Solomon used an almost identical construct in 1 Kings 2:37 when referring to Shimei:

> For on the day *[yom]* you go out and cross over the brook Kidron, you will know for certain that you shall surely *[muwth]* die *[muwth]*; your blood shall be on your own head (NASB).

This uses *yom* (day) and the dual *muwth* just as Genesis 2:17 did. In Genesis 2:17, *yom* referred to the action (eating) in the same way that *yom* refers the action here (go out and cross over). In neither case do they mean that was the particular day they would die, but the particular day they did what they weren't supposed to do. Solomon also understood that it would not be a death on that particular day, but that Shimei's days were numbered from that point. In other words, their (Adam and Shimei) actions on that day were what gave them the final death sentence — it was coming, and they would surely die as a result of their actions. Therefore, the day in Genesis 2:17 was referring to when they ate (disobeyed), and not the day they died.

Underneath a Solid Sky

Gary Vaterlaus

Does Genesis 1 teach the sky was solid?

Critics of the Bible have often said that the writings of Genesis reflect an "unscientific view" of the universe — one that reflected the cosmology of the ancient world. One of these criticisms centers on the Hebrew word *raqia* used in the creation account of Genesis 1. Several Bible versions, such as the New King James, translate this word as firmament:

> Then God said, "Let there be a firmament in the midst of the waters, and let it divide the waters from the waters." Thus God made the firmament, and divided the waters which were under the firmament from the waters which were above the firmament; and it was so. And God called the firmament Heaven. So the evening and the morning were the second day (Genesis 1:6–8).

The argument from these Bible critics is that the ancient Hebrews believed in a solid dome with the stars embedded in the dome. They say that the word firmament reflects the idea of firmness, and this reflects erroneous cosmology. Therefore, the Bible is not the inspired Word of God, and we don't need to listen to its teaching.

However, other versions of the Bible, such as the New American Standard, translate *raqia* as "expanse":

> Then God said, "Let there be an expanse in the midst of the waters, and let it separate the waters from the waters." God made the expanse, and separated the waters which were below the expanse from the waters which were above the expanse;

and it was so. God called the expanse heaven. And there was evening and there was morning, a second day (Genesis 1:6–8, NASB).

But which is the correct term to use? Where did the word *firmament* come from? The Septuagint (a Greek translation of the Hebrew Scriptures produced by Jewish scholars in the third century B.C. at the request of the Egyptian pharaoh) translates *raqia* into the Greek word *stereoma*, which connotes a solid structure. Apparently, the translators of the Septuagint were influenced by the Egyptian view of cosmology, which embraced the notion of the heavens being a stone vault (after all, they were doing their translation work in Egypt!). Later, this Greek connotation influenced Jerome to the extent that, when he produced his Latin Vulgate around A.D. 400, he used the Latin word *firmamentum* (meaning a strong or steadfast support). The King James translators merely transliterated this Latin word — and thus was born the firmament.

But what does the Hebrew word actually mean? The Hebrew noun *raqia* is derived from the verb *raqa*, which means "to spread abroad, stamp, or stretch." This word is used in the Old Testament in several places for the stamping out of metal into a sheet. Gold is a good example of this process. Gold is malleable, and people use a hammer or other tool to flatten and stretch it into very thin sheets (e.g., Numbers 8:4). However, we must remember that the context always determines the meaning of a word, not just the etymology of the word or how it may be used in other verses.

So, we need to ask ourselves, why did the author use this word to describe the expanse? What property did the author intend to be understood by the word *raqia*? It is possible that the author intended to get across the solid nature of the expanse. However, what if the intended understanding was the stretched-out nature of the *raqia* rather than its hardness? This understanding is consistent with the terminology of many other verses, such as Psalm 104:2 and Isaiah 40:22, which speak of the stretching out of the heavens. The Hebrew word used in these verses for heaven is not *raqia*, but *shamayim* (literally "heavens"). However, in Genesis 1:8, God explicitly calls the expanse "heaven," thus equating *raqia* with *shamayim*. If the stretched-out nature of the *raqia* is what is intended, then firmament may not be the best translation; expanse is more accurate.

The context of Genesis 1:6–8 and 14–22 makes it clear that Moses intended his readers to understand *raqia* simply as the sky (atmosphere and heavens or space) above the earth, as even the sun, moon, and stars were placed in them. In fact, in modern Hebrew *raqia* is the word used for sky, and there is no connotation of hardness.

Genesis 1 is perfectly worded for what the author wanted to communicate. It says nothing more than God created the sky and its constituent elements, while remaining completely silent about what those elements were. It really depends upon where one starts: if one starts with the presumption of a solid dome, one will read that into the text. However, if one starts with a modern conception of sky, the text permits that understanding as well, and hence, there is no contradiction.

Full of Meaning

Stacia McKeever

Why would God tell Adam and Eve to "replenish" the earth in Genesis 1:22 if they were the first humans?

> And God blessed them, and God said unto them, Be fruitful, and multiply, and replenish the earth, and subdue it: and have dominion over the fish of the sea, and over the fowl of the air, and over every living thing that moveth upon the earth (Genesis 1:28; KJV).

According to some, this verse in the King James Version indicates that Adam and Eve were to *refill* the planet, implying that that they weren't the first humans God created but were part of a "second creation." Many who accept the gap theory believe this. However, take a look at the same verse in the New King James Version.

> Then God blessed them, and God said to them, "Be fruitful and multiply; fill the earth and subdue it; have dominion over the fish of the sea, over the birds of the air, and over every living thing that moves on the earth" (Genesis 1:28).

The word *replenish* in the King James Version was used in the 17th century (when the King James Version was translated) to simply mean "fill." It expressed such ideas as to stock, fill, supply, or inhabit. Replenish is related to the word *replete*; being replete with happiness is being full with happiness. According to the Oxford English Dictionary, the first recorded use of the word replenish to mean "to fill again" occurred in 1612, one year after the King James Version was published. Furthermore, it was used in a poetic sense, and Genesis 1:28 is not poetry. The English word has changed meaning over the centuries so that the word replenish today generally means "refill."

Demolishing Contradictions

The original Hebrew word for replenish in Genesis 1:28 is *male*. This word simply means "fill" and is translated that way in the King James elsewhere (e.g., Genesis 1:22). So neither the Hebrew word nor the English word chosen by the King James Version translators meant, at that time, "refill." The translators' choice of *replenish* may have been meant to convey something akin to "fill up" (i.e., to "make replete [full]"), but they were certainly not trying to convey anything about another filling of the earth.

The New King James Version (and some other versions) correctly translates the word in today's parlance as "fill." This apparent "contradiction" is simply a translational issue — not an error in the original manuscripts.

My Three Sons

Bodie Hodge

Were Noah's sons born when he was 500 as Genesis 5:32 says or not as stated in Genesis 7:6 and Genesis 11:10?

The Bible indicates that Noah had three sons prior to the Flood (Genesis 6:10). Noah's sons were not all the same age, but let's first begin with Genesis 5:32:

> After Noah was 500 years old, he became the father of Shem, Ham and Japheth (Genesis 5:32; NIV).

This indicates that Noah was 500 or just over when his first son was born. Listings such as these are rarely an indication of ages but show that Noah *began* having children when he was 500 (Genesis 11:26). The listing of children often started with the most important one (through Shem we receive the blessing of Christ). We know the relative ages of each from Genesis 10:21 and Genesis 9:24.

> Sons were also born to Shem, whose older brother was Japheth; Shem was the ancestor of all the sons of Eber (Genesis 10:21; NIV).

> When Noah awoke from his wine and found out what his youngest son [Ham] had done to him (Genesis 9:24; NIV).

Genesis 10:21 indicates that Japheth was the oldest and was born when Noah was 500 years old. Ham is the youngest, as indicated in Genesis 9:24, after Ham's inappropriate actions to his father.

Therefore, Shem had to be born in between Japheth and Ham. Shem wasn't born as a triplet or twin of Japheth when Noah was 500, as shown by Genesis 7:6 and Genesis 11:10.

> Noah was six hundred years old when the floodwaters came on the earth (Genesis 7:6; NIV).

> This is the account of Shem. Two years after the flood, when Shem was 100 years old, he became the father of Arphaxad (Genesis 11:10; NIV).

So, Noah was 600 when the floodwaters came on the earth, and two years later Shem was 100. Therefore, Shem had to be born to Noah when he was 502. We are not sure of Ham's exact age in Scripture, but he had to be born after Shem. Thus, Genesis 5:32 introduces us to Noah's sons all together when Noah began having them, and other passages give more detail about their birth order and age.

Location, Location, Location

Bodie Hodge

Why do names of places appear in both the pre-Flood and post-Flood world? Does this refute a global Flood that should have destroyed such places?

When we read Genesis 6–9, it is obvious that there was a global Flood. So the alleged contradiction is that some pre-Flood place names reappear after the Flood. For example, table 1 illustrates the most common ones.

Table 1. Pre-Flood and Post-Flood References

Name	Bible Reference		Person
	Pre-Flood	Post-Flood	
Havilah	Genesis 2:11	Genesis 10:7, 29	Noah's grandson through Ham; Noah's great, great, great, great grandson through Shem
Cush	Genesis 2:13	Genesis 10:6	Noah's grandson through Ham
Asshur	Genesis 2:14 (NIV)	Genesis 10:22	Noah's grandson through Shem
Tigris	Genesis 2:14 (NIV)	Genesis 10:4	River in modern-day Iraq
Euphrates	Genesis 2:14	Genesis 15:18	River in modern-day Iraq

The answer to this conundrum is quite simple, but let's use some illustrations so that we can better understand this.

Demolishing Contradictions

Names of places often transfer. For example, Versailles, Illinois, was named for Versailles, Kentucky, when settlers moved from Kentucky into Illinois. And before that Versailles, Kentucky, was named for Versailles, France. If someone said to meet me in Versailles, you may have to ask "which one?"

Names of places often come from names of people as well. The land of Canaan was named form Noah's grandson Canaan. St. Louis, Missouri, was named for King Louis IX of France.

Names of people sometimes came from places. Consider the name London that many people today have and its origin as a city in England.

With this in mind, it should be fairly easy to see how names could easily have been transferred through the Flood. Ham's grandson was likely named after the land of Havilah. Cush was Ham's son, and Asshur was Shem's son. Noah, Ham, and Shem lived before the Flood and would have been aware of these regions. And of course, these names have gone on to become names of regions where some of these people settled after the dispersal of the Tower of Babel. Cush is modern-day Ethiopia, Asshur was where Assyria developed into a great nation, and so on.

For example, if I were to mention the "Thames River," most people would quickly think of a river in southern England. However, the state of Connecticut in the United States, as well as Ontario, Canada, each have a river named "Thames." When people settled in the Americas from Europe, they named some of these rivers for rivers they were familiar with. Why would we expect Noah and his descendants to do any differently? The Tigris and Euphrates that we know today in modern-day Iraq were named for the famous headwaters in the Garden of Eden.

There is no contradiction, but merely a situation of renaming new places, rivers, and people with previously used names.

The Order of Nations

Gary Vaterlaus

Do Genesis 10 and 11 contradict each other about the origin of nations and people groups?

The charge has been made that there is a contradiction in Genesis 10–11. The accusation is that if people had already spread around the world (as recorded in Genesis 10), fulfilling God's command, why was mankind judged with the confusion of languages as recorded in Genesis 11? This is actually an easy "contradiction" to clear up.

Genesis 10, often called "the Table of Nations," traces the origins of nations and people groups as they dispersed around the world after the Flood. It is a historical narrative of the descendants of Noah's three sons. That chapter concludes with this statement:

> These were the families of the sons of Noah, according to their generations, in their nations; and from these the nations were divided on the earth after the flood (Genesis 10:32).

After the descendants of each of the sons of Noah are mentioned, the text says that they were dispersed "according to their families, according to their languages" (Genesis 10:5, 20, 31). So, if Noah and his sons all spoke the same language, where did all of these other languages come from? Genesis 11 gives us the answer.

These groups of people did not willingly and obediently separate to fill the earth. Rather, we learn in Genesis 11:1–9 why these families separated from each other and how it came to be that there were so many languages in the world.

There is no contradiction here; Moses merely put the effect before the cause. Genesis 10 gives an overview, and then Genesis 11 fills in the details. You often find the same technique in other history books. One chapter might contain an overview of World

Demolishing Contradictions

War I — along with a list of major events. But the very next chapter might detail what the world was like in the years before the war and what events led up to it.

There may also be another reason why the order of these two events is switched. Keith Krell explains:

> The actual outworking of the genealogies of Genesis 10 occurs after the events at the Tower of Babel (cf. 11:1 with 10:5, 20, 31). This interspersal of narrative (11:1–9) separates the two genealogies of Shem (10:21–31; 11:10–26), paving the way for the particular linkage between the Terah (Abraham) clan and the Shemite lineage (11:27). The story of the tower also looks ahead by anticipating the role that Abram (12:1–3) will play in restoring the blessing to the dispersed nations. By placing the Tower of Babel incident just prior to the stories of Abram and his descendants, the biblical writer is suggesting, in the first place, that post-flood humanity is as wicked as pre-flood humanity. Rather than sending something as devastating as a flood to annihilate mankind, however, God now places His hope in a covenant with Abraham as a powerful solution to humanity's sinfulness. This problem (Genesis 11) and solution (Genesis 12) are brought into immediate juxtaposition, and the forcefulness of this structural move would have been lost had Genesis 10 intervened between the two.[4]

---

4. Keith Krell, "The Spread of the Nations: Genesis 10:1–11:26," http://bible.org/seriespage/spread-nations-genesis-101-1126 (accessed Sep. 16, 2010).

A Lot of Relationships

Roger Patterson

Is Lot Abraham's nephew or his brother?

> This is the genealogy of Terah: Terah begot Abram, Nahor, and Haran. Haran begot Lot (Genesis 11:27).

> And Terah took his son Abram and his grandson Lot, the son of Haran, and his daughter-in-law Sarai, his son Abram's wife, and they went out with them from Ur of the Chaldeans to go to the land of Canaan; and they came to Haran and dwelt there (Genesis 11:31).

> Then Abram took Sarai his wife and Lot his brother's son, and all their possessions that they had gathered, and the people whom they had acquired in Haran, and they departed to go to the land of Canaan. So they came to the land of Canaan (Genesis 12:5).

> So Abram said to Lot, "Let's not have any quarrelling between you and me, or between your herdsmen and mine, for we are brothers" (Genesis 13:8; NIV).

The apparent contradiction comes from the translation of the Hebrew word *awkh*. This word can mean brother, half-brother, relative, partner, or something with a resemblance. As in our language, the contexts in which words are used determine their meaning. The clear passages lay out the genealogy of the sons of Terah. Genesis 11:27 makes it clear that Lot is Haran's son, not Terah's. This is confirmed by verse 11:31 and 12:5. The apparent conflict comes when Abram appeals to Lot on the basis of their close relationship. He refers to Abram as a brother, but his appeal is to their bond as close relatives.

Demolishing Contradictions

Even in our culture, the term *brother* is used to represent people with a bond through civic clubs and military service. Paul referred to Timothy (as well as many other believers) as a brother (e.g., 2 Corinthians 1:1; Colossians 1:1). Indeed, that term applies to all believers — we are brothers and sisters in Christ. If one were to have a brother (sharing mother and father) who has not repented and put his trust in Christ for salvation, he would not be a brother in Christ. Depending on the context, he would be both a brother and not a brother.

The context makes it clear that Lot was both Abram's nephew and his brother: his nephew by actual relationship, yet a brother as a member of the family of Terah.

Left in the Dust

Gary Vaterlaus

Do snakes really eat dust like Genesis says?

Some people try to discredit Genesis by saying snakes don't eat dust, as Genesis 3:14 claims and that, therefore, the Bible is in error.

After the serpent deceived Eve, God cursed it, saying, "On your belly you will go, and dust you will eat all the days of your life." Although we can't know for sure that the serpent referred to in Genesis 1 really was the same as a snake today, many people use this verse as a reason not to take Genesis literally, since snakes don't *eat* dust.

Many have responded to this charge by pointing out that a snake has an organ located in the front of the roof of its mouth that functions as a chemical receptor. The Jacobson's organ helps the snake smell. As a snake's forked tongue darts out to sense its surroundings, it, at least occasionally, licks the ground or picks up dust particles. Once the snake pulls in its tongue, it inserts the tips of its forked tongue into the two openings of the Jacobson's organ, where the particles are identified and analyzed. The snake's brain can "read" the smells and tastes from its tongue. So, in a way, snakes really do eat dust.

But is this really what God had in mind when He cursed the serpent? Probably not. Let's look at Genesis 3:14–15 for the context:

> So the LORD God said to the serpent,
> "Because you have done this,
> You are cursed more than all cattle,
> And more than every beast of the field;
> On your belly you shall go,
> And you shall eat dust
> All the days of your life.

> And I will put enmity
> Between you and the woman,
> And between your seed and her Seed;
> He shall bruise your head,
> And you shall bruise His heel."

Notice that the serpent's curse included crawling on its belly, eating dust, bruising the heel of the woman's Seed, and the Seed bruising the head of the serpent. Most theologians have recognized verse 15 as the protoevangelium ("first gospel"). God, here, prophesies the coming of the Messiah, Jesus, the one who would die for our sins and rise again, defeating Satan. The bruising of the heel and the bruising of the head are obviously symbolic language, pointing to a greater reality. Recognizing this in no way violates the historical genre of Genesis: the symbolic language is still couched within a largely literal framework.

So did God curse the animal or Satan? It appears He cursed both of them. Throughout the Scriptures, God commonly speaks to the vessel and then to Satan. Here are a few examples.

In Ezekiel 27–28, the Word of the Lord was said to Tyre itself (Ezekiel 27:2), then to the ruler of Tyre (Ezekiel 28:2), and then a lament beginning in Ezekiel 28:11 to the "king of Tyre." This one was specifically directed to the one influencing the king of Tyre — Satan.

Jesus rebuked Peter and then spoke to Satan when He influenced Peter in Mark 8:33.

In Isaiah 14 God spoke to the king of Babylon and in some parts, to Satan, who was influencing him.

This concept of speaking directly to Satan while he is influencing someone is nothing uncommon. So there is no stretch to understand that the Lord is speaking to the serpent *and* Satan in Genesis 3. Genesis 3:14 is said to the serpent, and then Genesis 3:15 is said to Satan, who is influencing the serpent.

The curse pronounced upon the serpent of "eating the dust" results in it now crawling on its belly in the dust. It used to be like one of the "cattle" and "beast of the field" (Genesis 3:1, 14), but now will crawl on its belly and eat dirt. More importantly, this imagery of eating dust is symbolic of a creature low, despicable, abhorrent, and degraded. In Micah 7:16–17, God prophesies of a time when the nations will come crawling to Him:

> The nations shall see and be ashamed of all their might;
> They shall put their hand over their mouth;
> Their ears shall be deaf.
> They shall lick the dust like a serpent;
> They shall crawl from their holes like snakes of the earth.
> They shall be afraid of the LORD our God,
> And shall fear because of You.

A proper understanding of the context (literary, historical, and theological) helps us understand what God meant when He cursed the serpent. There is no contradiction here, but rather a wonderful promise of victory by a risen Savior.

Two Creation Accounts?

Paul F. Taylor

Do Genesis 1 and 2 give different accounts?

The claim goes that there are two creation accounts: Genesis 1 and 2 give different accounts. In chapter 1, man and woman are created at the same time after the creation of the animals. In chapter 2, the animals are created after people.

This apparent contradiction is best illustrated by looking at Genesis 2:19.

> Out of the ground the LORD God formed every beast of the field and every bird of the air, and brought them to Adam to see what he would call them.

The language appears to suggest that God made the animals after making Adam and then He brought the animals to Adam. However, in Genesis 1, we have an account of God creating animals *and then* creating men and women.

The difficulty with Genesis 2:19 lies with the use of the word *formed*. The same style is read in the KJV.

> And out of the ground the LORD God formed every beast of the field, and every fowl of the air; and brought them unto Adam to see what he would call them.

The NIV has a subtly different rendition.

> Now the LORD God had formed out of the ground all the beasts of the field and all the birds of the air. He brought them to the man to see what he would name them.

The NIV suggests a different way of viewing the first two chapters of Genesis. Genesis 2 does not suggest a chronology. That is why the NIV suggests using the style "the Lord God *had formed* out of the ground all the beasts of the fields." Therefore, the animals being brought to Adam had already been made and were not being brought to him immediately after their creation. Interestingly, Tyndale agrees with the NIV — and Tyndale's translation predates the KJV.

> The Lord God had made of the earth all manner of beasts of the field and all manner fowls of the air.

Tyndale and the NIV are correct on this verse because the verb in the sentence can be translated as *pluperfect* rather than *perfect*. The pluperfect tense can be considered as the past of the past — that is to say, in a narration set in the past, the event to which the narration refers is already further in the past. Once the pluperfect is taken into account, the perceived contradiction completely disappears.

By the Light of the Moon

John Upchurch

Does Genesis 1:15 say that the moon emits its own light?

In Genesis we read:

> Let them [sun and moon] be for lights in the expanse of the heavens to give [emit] light on the earth (Genesis 1:15; NASB).

Over the years, a number of skeptics have pointed to this verse to claim that if the Bible were really the inerrant Word of God, it wouldn't make such a basic mistake as saying the moon emits light. The moon has not and does not — as far as we know — emit any sort of light. Instead, our rocky satellite simply reflects light from the sun.

While there have been a few claims that the moon does generate its own light through thermoluminescence, there really is no need to search for such exotic explanations as far as this verse is involved. In fact, a look at our own modern lexicon gives us the answer to this supposed contradiction.

Consider for a moment how earth-centric our discussions are. We say that the sun rises and sets, even though we know that the earth actually revolves around the sun and rotates on its axis. We say that the stars "come out" at night, even though we know they're always there — just hidden by the brighter sunlight. Our point of reference determines how we discuss what we see.

To us, the moon *does* emit light onto the earth. The sun's light strikes the surface of the moon and reflects back at the earth. Notice that the Genesis text does not say or suggest that the moon generates its own light. In fact, the point is not the source of the light;

the point is the impact that the lights have on earth. One "governs" the day, and the lesser one "governs" the night (Genesis 1:16). If the moon were a light *source* — instead of simply a light — there would likely be no night at all for it to govern.

We can easily demonstrate this concept when we imagine someone reflecting light into our eyes from a mirror. The mirror is not the source of the light, but it does emit a powerful beam that can momentarily blind — something even biblio-skeptics would have to admit. And when such a beam is blinding someone, it is doubtful that *how* the light reaches the person's eyes would matter so much as the fact that it is.

Taking this verse out of context also makes it seem much more damaging, but when we step back (cf. Genesis 1:14–18), we understand more about the purpose of this passage. Other than providing light, God created the sun and moon to mark the seasons, days, and years, which they do quite well. Notice that the Bible does not provide detailed schematics and charts on how this works, since God gave humans the ability to discover these through observational science. The purpose here is not to explain all the details (though it is factually accurate and *not* a simplified metaphor for "primitive humans"); the purpose is to give an overview and the reasons why God did what He did. Thus, the description of the moon as giving light is not detailed, but it is quite accurate.

The real message to take from this passage is that God created two spectacular heavenly bodies that are constant reminders of His amazing power. This verse lets us (earth-centric humans) know exactly what God intended: how the sun and moon came to be and why He created them.

Exodus – Deuteronomy

A Time to Kill

Roger Patterson

Is it okay to kill, like David killing Goliath or Joshua eliminating Canaanites? Or is killing forbidden?

"You shall not murder" (Exodus 20:13; NASB).

"If the thief is found breaking in, and he is struck so that he dies, there shall be no guilt for his bloodshed" (Exodus 22:2).

"Whoever curses his God shall bear his sin. And whoever blasphemes the name of the LORD shall surely be put to death" (Leviticus 24:15–16).

"Whoever kills any man shall surely be put to death" (Leviticus 24:17).

So David prevailed over the Philistine with a sling and a stone, and struck the Philistine and killed him (1 Samuel 17:50).

In order to answer this apparent contradiction, we must make a distinction between killing someone and committing murder. Murder is the *unlawful* taking of a life, while killing may be lawful or unlawful. The establishment of capital punishment actually extends back to the Noahic Covenant when God declared, "Surely for your lifeblood I will demand a reckoning; from the hand of every beast I will require it, and from the hand of man. From the hand of every man's brother I will require the life of man. Whoever sheds man's blood, by man his blood shall be shed; for in the image of God He made man" (Genesis 9:5–6).

Even before this, Cain was afraid of the other members of his family seeking to kill him after he had murdered his brother Abel (Genesis 4:13–15).[5] In the cases outlined in Scripture, taking the

---

5. The Lord did protect Cain by placing a mark on him to prevent others from taking his life. After the Flood, things changed.

life of another in the name of justice was not murder. The question poses a false dilemma in that killing does not have to be always right or always wrong — God has provided qualifications.

Because man is made in the image of God, the death of a human is not taken lightly. In the laws given to Israel through Moses, those sins that were worthy of death were detailed. Leviticus 19 is one such place where these commands are given. Since these are commands directly from God and God cannot lie, we understand that there must be no contradiction in the commands. Those who committed sexual sins were to be justly killed, but only upon the clear affirmation of their crime established by witnesses.

As the author of the first five books of the Bible, Moses would not have written contradictory ideas. If we allow for killing to be wrong in every case, when a person carried out capital punishment, as commanded by God, they would have to be killed for the taking of a life. Then their life would be demanded, and so on until humanity was left with one. Extending the logic allows us to see how absurd the claim of a contradiction truly is.

The Bible provides many circumstances under which the taking of a life is legally allowed by Scripture. Killing another person in an act of self-defense (Exodus 22:2) was permitted with no consequences. There are examples of God calling the people to war against other nations to punish them for their sins. When Joshua led the children of Israel into the Promised Land, God commanded the Israelites to utterly destroy the idolatrous peoples who inhabited the land (Deuteronomy 20:16–17). A list of their sins can be found in Leviticus 18, including incest, murdering children, and so on. When God called Israel to war against those in the Promised Land, then He was permitting the killing in this situation, making men His agents of justice, as in the case with capital punishment.

The killing of Goliath by the young David was, likewise, justified in the eyes of God. In fact, David was angered by the way that Goliath blasphemed God and met him in battle. David did not trust in himself, but in the Lord to deliver Goliath into his hands.

This is an example of continuance of the war the Israelites had been engaged in with the inhabitants of the Promised Land, as directed by God.

God repeatedly chose war and capital punishment as a way to bring judgment on peoples and individuals who were acting in defiance of His will by doing great sin. He ordained the killing as a punishment to accomplish His purposes in the world.

This should give an idea of seriousness of sin. In the eyes of a perfect and holy God, one sin is worthy of death (Genesis 2:17). Since we are all sinners, we are all under the death sentence already. In essence, we are all on "death row," and those who murder or do other terrible sins as described in Scripture simply had their wait on "death row" shortened.

God hates sin, especially those that lead to any situation where a human life is lost. His holy nature and subsequent hatred of sin make the taking of a life acceptable only in the rarest of cases. We should never seek to minimize the taking of a life — a life made in the image of God. Remember that taking a life for justifiable reasons is only necessary because we live in a world of sin. The perfect creation would not have required death for any reason.

Bats of a Feather

Bodie Hodge

Did Moses make an error when he called a bat a bird?

Moses, who was one of the most-learned in Egypt, has been attacked in several cases to undermine biblical authority. This is another of those attacks to get people to doubt that God was speaking through Moses. Let's evaluate such a claim in more detail. The passage reads:

> These are the birds you are to detest and not eat because they are detestable: the eagle, the vulture, the black vulture, the red kite, any kind of black kite, any kind of raven, the horned owl, the screech owl, the gull, any kind of hawk, the little owl, the cormorant, the great owl, the white owl, the desert owl, the osprey, the stork, any kind of heron, the hoopoe and the bat (Leviticus 11:13–19; NIV).

The Hebrew word for bird is actually *owph* which means "fowl/winged creature."[6] The word *owph* simply means "to fly" or "has a wing." So the word includes birds, bats, and even flying insects. The alleged problem appears due to translation of *owph* as "bird." Birds are included in the word *owph*, but *owph* is not limited to birds. This shows that translators aren't always perfect when handling the inerrant Word of God.

---

6. F. Brown, S. Driver, and C. Briggs, *The Brown-Driver-Brigg Hebrew and English Lexicon*, 9th printing (Peabody, MA: Hendrickson Publishers, 2005), p. 773.

Two Missing Legs

Bodie Hodge

Did Moses say that insects have only four legs?

In Leviticus11, Moses lists several animals that were clean and others that were not. In other words, it is a list of some what the Israelites were allowed to eat, when it comes to animals. In verses 20–23, some skeptics of the Bible believe Moses made a big mistake. It says:

> All flying insects that creep on all fours shall be an abomination to you. Yet these you may eat of every flying insect that creeps on all fours: those which have jointed legs above their feet with which to leap on the earth. These you may eat: the locust after its kind, the destroying locust after its kind, the cricket after its kind, and the grasshopper after its kind. But all other flying insects which have four feet shall be an abomination to you (Leviticus 11:20–23).

Leviticus 11:21 indicates that the hind jumping legs are not included in the four "walking" or "creeping" feet. The feet are the four front limbs used for walking and look the same. The back two limbs are primarily for long hops. Although today people lump them all together and say there are six legs, the Bible distinguished them here. The Bible referred to them in *more* detail than perhaps expected. Notice how the feet and legs are separated in the verses and referred to separately. The Bible is being very precise as to distinguish the front four from the back two. So there is no contradiction at all:

4 walking legs + 2 hind hopping legs = 6 total legs

Leviticus 11:20–23 refers only to the insects with these specific feet-leg combinations that have wings.[7] Now, I know you're wondering . . . did any Israelites actually eat these insects? Look up Matthew 3:4 and Mark 1:6!

---

7. Leviticus 11:41–43 excludes other insects (i.e., those that walk on six legs, arachnids, and myriapods).

Dead Man Writing

Roger Patterson

How could Moses be the author of Deuteronomy when his obituary is listed as the last chapter?

> Then Moses went up from the plains of Moab to Mount Nebo, to the top of Pisgah, which is across from Jericho. And the LORD showed him all the land of Gilead as far as Dan. . . . So Moses the servant of the LORD died there in the land of Moab, according to the word of the LORD. And He buried him in a valley in the land of Moab, opposite Beth Peor; but no one knows his grave to this day. Moses was one hundred and twenty years old when he died. His eyes were not dim nor his natural vigor diminished. . . . (Deuteronomy 34:1–7).

Moses is considered the author of the first five books of the Bible; the Pentateuch (Deuteronomy 31:24). Liberal scholars have rejected this claim, and theories abound as to the "true" authorship. Despite the detractors, the life and death of Moses are contained within these books, along with the account of the creation of the universe and the calling of the chosen people through Abraham, Isaac, and Jacob (Israel).

After wandering through the wilderness following the Exodus, the Children of Israel are poised at the edge of the Promised Land. At this time the authority of leadership held by Moses was transferred to Joshua (Deuteronomy 31:23). Joshua was to lead the nation into their new homeland without the company of Moses.

> Then the LORD said to him, "This is the land of which I swore to give Abraham, Isaac, and Jacob, saying, 'I will give it to your descendants.' I have caused you to see it with your eyes, but you shall not cross over there" (Deuteronomy 34:4).

After having seen the Promised Land, Moses died and was buried by God (Deuteronomy 34:5–6). If Moses was dead, then how could he be considered the author of Deuteronomy?

At the time of the writing, books were contained on scrolls. The ending of one book and the beginning of the next were not clearly delineated. In modern translations, there are many instances where the last verse is considered the first verse of the next chapter in the Jewish text. This does not mean that there is an error, but that the demarcations are different.

Likewise, the last chapter of Deuteronomy could as easily be considered the first chapter of Joshua without harming the integrity of the text. This is one possible solution to the inferred contradiction.

Another possibility is that having recorded the final words of blessing in Deuteronomy 33:29, another writer completed the story of Moses after his death. Being divinely inspired (2 Timothy 3:16–17), the author noted these last activities of Moses and placed them in the records. Exactly who this author was is a matter of dispute. Whether Joshua, Ezra, Eliazar, or another, the account simply closes out the life of Moses.

Whether we should rearrange the chapters or ascribe a different author to that small portion, there is no contradiction in the text. No truth of Scripture is altered by either of these resolutions to the apparent problem. If, upon your death, someone were to take your journal or personal memoirs and add a short description of your death, you would still be considered the author of the biography.

Too Close for Comfort

Gary Vaterlaus

Does God both bless and condemn marriages between close relations?

> And Abraham said, "Because I thought, surely the fear of God is not in this place; and they will kill me on account of my wife. But indeed she is truly my sister. She is the daughter of my father, but not the daughter of my mother; and she became my wife" (Genesis 20:11–12).

> "Cursed is the one who lies with his sister, the daughter of his father or the daughter of his mother." And all the people shall say, "Amen!" (Deuteronomy 27:22, also see Leviticus 18:6–9).

These two passages, to some, present quite a contradiction. Genesis tells us that Abraham, a man blessed by God, married his half-sister, while Moses in Deuteronomy tells the Israelites that anyone who lies with his sister shall be cursed. So is this a contradiction in the Bible? Not at all!

To understand why, we need to start at the beginning with Adam and Eve. We don't know how many children Adam and Eve had, but the Bible makes it clear that they had other "sons and daughters" in addition to Abel, Cain, and Seth (Genesis 5:4). So, for the human population to increase, and for them to be obedient to God's command to be fruitful and multiply, brother and sister had to get married. There were no others around! But doesn't this violate God's commands that prohibit close relations marrying? Certainly not.

We need to keep in mind that the Law of Moses wasn't given until around 1440 B.C., more than 2,500 years after creation and more than 400 years after Abraham's time. So why did God institute laws against marrying close relatives? The following section from the chapter "Cain's Wife — Who Was She?" in *The New Answers Book 1* explains why:

> The more closely related two people are, the more likely it is that they will have similar mistakes in their genes, inherited from the same parents. Therefore, brother and sister are likely to have similar mistakes in their genetic material. If there were to be a union between these two that produces offspring, children would inherit one set of genes from each of their parents. Because the genes probably have similar mistakes, the mistakes pair together and result in deformities in the children.
>
> . . . However, this fact of present-day life did not apply to Adam and Eve. When the first two people were created, they were perfect. Everything God made was "very good" (Genesis 1:31). That means their genes were perfect—no mistakes. But when sin entered the world because of Adam (Genesis 3:6), God cursed the world so that the perfect creation then began to degenerate, that is, suffer death and decay (Romans 8:22). Over a long period of time, this degeneration would have resulted in all sorts of mistakes occurring in the genetic material of living things.
>
> . . . By the time of Moses (about 2,500 years later), degenerative mistakes would have accumulated to such an extent in the human race that it would have been necessary for God to bring in the laws forbidding brother-sister (and close relative) marriage (Leviticus 18–20).[8]

So, once again, we see that there are no contradictions in the Scriptures when we take the time to study them in their proper historical and theological context.

---

8. Ken Ham, editor, *The New Answers Book 1* (Green Forest, AR: Master Books, 2006), p. 72–73.

Face to Face

Bodie Hodge

Can God be seen face to face (Genesis 32:30; Exodus 33:11) or not (Exodus 33:20; John 1:18; 1 John 4:12)?

The relevant passages are:

> So Jacob called the name of the place Peniel: "For I have seen God face to face, and my life is preserved" (Genesis 32:30).

> So the LORD spoke to Moses face to face, as a man speaks to his friend. And he would return to the camp, but his servant Joshua the son of Nun, a young man, did not depart from the tabernacle (Exodus 33:11).

> But He said, "You cannot see My face; for no man shall see Me, and live" (Exodus 33:20).

> No one has seen God at any time. The only begotten Son, who is in the bosom of the Father, He has declared Him (John 1:18).

> No one has seen God at any time. If we love one another, God abides in us, and His love has been perfected in us (1 John 4:12).

At first, one might think this is among the greatest of alleged contradictions, for its form mimics the Law of Non-contradiction. A contradictionist may say, "We've got a good one on you because A cannot equal not-A, and these verses show that God can both be seen face to face and not." But sometimes people fail to realize the rest of the Law of Non-contradiction that states, "A cannot equal not-A at the same time and in the same relationship."

Usually when I see two verses allegedly in contradiction so close together in context (e.g., Exodus 33:11 and Exodus 33:20), then the context will be significant in helping us reveal there is a different time or relationship, hence not in contradiction. And this is exactly the case here. Between Exodus 33:11 and Exodus 33:20, Moses and the Lord are speaking, but a change in relationship occurs in verses 18 and 19. The greater context of this is shown:

> [17] So the LORD said to Moses, "I will also do this thing that you have spoken; for you have found grace in My sight, and I know you by name." [18] And he said, "Please, show me Your glory." [19] Then He said, "I will make all My goodness pass before you, and I will proclaim the name of the LORD before you. I will be gracious to whom I will be gracious, and I will have compassion on whom I will have compassion." [20] But He said, "You cannot see My face; for no man shall see Me, and live."

At this point, the relationship has changed to signify that Moses asked to see the Lord *in His glory!* Not the typical face to face as revealed to sinful humans and as had already been revealed to Moses. Then the Lord informed Moses that if any man saw Him face to face (in His glory), then they would die (see also 1 Corinthians 1:29).

The context of John 1 reveals a similar situation of God in His glory:

> [15] John bore witness of Him and cried out, saying, "This was He of whom I said, 'He who comes after me is preferred before me, for He was before me.' " [16] And of His fullness we have all received, and grace for grace. [17] For the law was given through Moses, but grace and truth came through Jesus Christ. [18] No one has seen God at any time. The only begotten Son, who is in the bosom of the Father, He has declared Him.

John discusses God's fullness (hence, His glory) in verse 16 and points out that no one has seen God (in this fullness), but Christ, who declares Him (who was God in humbled flesh, according to Philippians 2:8 and the earlier context of John 1). The verse in 1 John 4:12 restates John's previous statement and is, thus, not in contradiction, but consistent as well.

Hence, there is no contradiction, as God can speak face to face with men, but not while in all His glory; otherwise, sinful man would die.

Change of Heart

Stacia McKeever

Does God change His mind?

> "For I am the LORD, I do not change; therefore you are not consumed, O sons of Jacob" (Malachi 3:6).

> God is not a man, that He should lie, nor a son of man, that He should repent. Has He said, and will He not do? Or has He spoken, and will He not make it good? (Numbers 23:19).

> And also the Strength of Israel will not lie nor relent. For He is not a man, that He should relent (1 Samuel 15:29).

It's clear from verses such as these that God is immutable — His nature and character do not change. He is the same yesterday, today, and forever (Hebrews 13:8). Other passages, such as those below, speak of God relenting in His judgment on a nation or group of people, mainly as the result of the pleas of an intercessor or repentance on the part of the nation. Does this pose a contradiction?

> So the LORD relented from the harm which He said He would do to His people (Exodus 32:14).

> Perhaps everyone will listen and turn from his evil way, that I may relent concerning the calamity which I purpose to bring on them because of the evil of their doings (Jeremiah 26:3).

> Now therefore, amend your ways and your doings, and obey the voice of the LORD your God; then the LORD will relent concerning the doom that He has pronounced against you (Jeremiah 26:13).

> Did Hezekiah king of Judah and all Judah ever put him to death? Did he not fear the LORD and seek the LORD's favor? And the LORD relented concerning the doom which He had pronounced against them. But we are doing great evil against ourselves (Jeremiah 26:19).

Then God saw their works, that they turned from their evil way; and God relented from the disaster that He had said He would bring upon them, and He did not do it (Jonah 3:10).

From the Bible, we know that God, in His holiness and righteousness, must punish sin and that His decreed punishment for sin is death (Genesis 2:15–17; Romans 6:23). Yet we also know that God is full of grace and abounding in mercy, forgiving the repentant of their sins (Exodus 34:6–7). The balance between these two aspects of God's nature may be best summed up in this passage from Jeremiah:

The instant I speak concerning a nation and concerning a kingdom, to pluck up, to pull down, and to destroy it, if that nation against whom I have spoken turns from its evil, I will relent of the disaster that I thought to bring upon it. And the instant I speak concerning a nation and concerning a kingdom, to build and to plant it, if it does evil in My sight so that it does not obey My voice, then I will relent concerning the good with which I said I would benefit it (Jeremiah 18:7–10).

Expressing Emotions

The following passages have also been used to accuse God of changing His mind.

And the LORD was sorry that He had made man on the earth, and He was grieved in His heart (Genesis 6:6).

"I greatly regret that I have set up Saul as king, for he has turned back from following Me, and has not performed My commandments." And it grieved Samuel, and he cried out to the LORD all night (1 Samuel 15:11).

Nowhere in Scripture does it indicate that God is not emotive. In fact, emotions are often ascribed to God in anthropomorphic or anthropopathic language. The Bible describes God's actions and emotions in terms of human actions and emotions.

Passages such as the two above simply show the emotional reactions God has to sin in those He created in His image. They aren't expressions of, "I didn't do that right the first time; guess I better figure out something else to do." Instead, God is grieving over disobedience and wickedness: a response that we should all have to sin. Again, this doesn't indicate a change in His nature or character; in fact, it is His holy nature that demands this response of grief. As finite, created beings, we understand that there are consequences associated with our moral decisions. The Bible is quite clear on that matter (Galatians 6:7). Yet, the "relenting" of God is, in many cases, the voice of compassion and mercy from a longsuffering God extended to sinful creatures in need of grace.

God's character does not change. However, He can change how He chooses to respond to an individual or nation's actions.

Joshua – Malachi

Slaughter at Jericho

Steve Fazekas

Could the loving God of the New Testament order the complete destruction of the inhabitants of Jericho found in the Old Testament?

The massacre of the inhabitants who occupied the fortified city-outpost known as Jericho can raise many questions in the mind of the careful reader. The higher critic has claimed for many years there was a conflict between the Bible and current archaeological data and that the claimed historicity of the sacred text was merely exaggerated colorful myth. Some liberal thinkers have viewed the Jehovah of the Old Testament as a deity who required appeasement and blood sacrifice to satisfy his capricious lust, while the New Testament god, in their view, is all about love, acceptance, and toleration. Then, the atheist uses the Bible to "prove" to the Christian that the God of his Scripture is a warmonger and the murderer of innocent women and children, and even if He did exist, He would remain unworthy of the worship and adoration required to satisfy His huge ego.

Even many an ardent Bible believer has felt some uneasiness at the unashamed transparency of the sacred text. Along with this comes the struggle to reconcile the relationship between a good and benevolent God and the obvious presence of evil in the world, especially as it relates to the death of women and children.

Recall the youthful gusto with which many have sung the traditional American spiritual.

> Joshua fit de battle of Jericho,
> Jericho, Jericho,
> Joshua fit de battle of Jericho,
> An de walls come a tumbling down.

Demolishing Contradictions

Of course, in Sunday school, as we marched around the chairs and pretended to blow the ram-horns, we were definitely on the side of the "good guys." On the other hand, Jericho and its inhabitants were the villains who deserved to lose their city, though we didn't know why. Only much later did we come to realize there was a sober side to this deadly dance, which gave new face and fresh meaning to our childish play.

Let us consider the text as it reads in the Authorized Version of the Bible.

> And they utterly destroyed all that was in the city, both man
> and woman, young and old, and ox, and sheep, and ass, with
> the edge of the sword (Joshua 6:21; KJV).

Try as we might, there is no way we can dodge the dilemma by laying the event at the feet of an overly zealous Joshua leading a nomadic army of marauding, misguided Israelites. Nor can we sweep it under the rug by allowing for some kind of modified divine permission or restraint, which might absolve God from any direct culpability. The fact remains; it was a carefully calculated act with a specific goal in mind. Jehovah ordered it (Deuteronomy 7:2), and Joshua did it (Joshua 6:21).

The qualifier in this saga seems to be what is referred to in Genesis 15:16 as the "iniquity of the Amorites." The nations that occupied Canaan had become so hideously debauched, so degenerate in custom and practice, that the judgment of God became imminent. We are told in the Mosaic account that God is preparing to act and His longsuffering is about to end.

> For the land has become defiled, therefore I have brought its
> punishment upon it, so the land has spewed out its inhabit-
> ants (Leviticus 18:25; NASB).

In the larger context of the writings of Moses, the Amorites are viewed by Jehovah as representative of the whole of Palestine. Further, it was as if they had become so saturated with corruption that the very earth itself spit them out.

Recent textual discoveries in Ugarit confirm the Scripture record of centuries filled with idolatry, sodomy, bestiality, sorcery, and child sacrifice. Consequently, each generation had polluted the next with idolatry, perversion, and blood. We must not read Deuteronomy 18:9–12 with an emotionless indifference in the way that some would read yesterday's news. Parents offered up their children to the god Molech by fire. Child sacrifice is more than an unfortunate, ancient tribal custom. It is a hideous, twisted ritual conducted by men who have reprobated themselves into beasts. Then again, the customs of Canaan are not really a quantum leap from ancient religious ritual to our current indulgence of "a woman's right to choose," are they?

The problem of Jericho is easily solved. God has revealed Himself to us in the Bible just as He is. His self-revelation to Moses (see Exodus 34:6–7) is very revealing:

> And Jehovah passed by before him and proclaimed, Jehovah, Jehovah, a God merciful and gracious, slow to anger and abundant in lovingkindness and truth; keeping lovingkindness for thousands, forgiving iniquity and transgression and sin; and that will by no means clear the guilty, visiting the iniquity of the fathers upon the children, and upon the children's children . . . (ASV).

Can we not see that God's disposition is showcased in His long-suffering, equity, mercy, and patience? He never acts in a knee-jerk, capricious manner. Yet at the same time, God reserves the right to be God, doing as He chooses when He wills and with universal authority over His creation. Even as he pleaded for God to spare the inhabitants of Sodom and Gomorrah, Abraham declared, "Shall not the judge of all the earth do right?" (Genesis 18:25). So the answer to the problem lies bound up in the character of God as revealed in Scripture. Is there ever a time when divine genocide is justified? The answer must be yes, because the judge of the whole earth always does what is right. Scripture makes it abundantly clear that in time the longsuffering of God will transform itself into judgment if the warnings are not heeded.

A.W. Tozer in *The Knowledge of the Holy* says it well:

> Before the Christian church goes into eclipse anywhere, there must first be the corrupting of her simple basic theology. She simply gets a wrong answer to the question, "What is God like?" Though she may continue to cling to a sound nominal creed, her practical working creed has become false. The masses of her adherents come to believe that God is different from what He actually is; and that is heresy of the most insidious and deadly kind.[9]

Here are words from the Apostle Paul challenging us to think biblically about the nature and character of God. "Behold then the goodness and severity of God" (Romans 11:22; ASV).

---

9. A.W. Tozer, *The Knowledge of the Holy* (New York: Harper San Francisco, 1992).

Cut in Half

Roger Patterson

Was Solomon really going to cut a baby in half?

Let's take a look at the context to get a grasp on the situation here:

> Now two women who were harlots came to the king, and stood before him. And one woman said, "O my lord, this woman and I dwell in the same house; and I gave birth while she was in the house. Then it happened, the third day after I had given birth, that this woman also gave birth. And we were together; no one was with us in the house, except the two of us in the house. And this woman's son died in the night, because she lay on him. So she arose in the middle of the night and took my son from my side, while your maid-servant slept, and laid him in her bosom, and laid her dead child in my bosom. And when I rose in the morning to nurse my son, there he was, dead. But when I had examined him in the morning, indeed, he was not my son whom I had borne."
>
> Then the other woman said, "No! But the living one is my son, and the dead one is your son."
>
> And the first woman said, "No! But the dead one is your son, and the living one is my son." Thus they spoke before the king.
>
> And the king said, "The one says, 'This is my son, who lives, and your son is the dead one'; and the other says, 'No! But your son is the dead one, and my son is the living one.'" Then the king said, "Bring me a sword." So they brought a sword before the king. And the king said, "Divide the living child in two, and give half to one, and half to the other."
>
> Then the woman whose son was living spoke to the king, for she yearned with compassion for her son; and she said, "O my lord, give her the living child, and by no means kill him!"

> But the other said, "Let him be neither mine nor yours, but divide him."
>
> So the king answered and said, "Give the first woman the living child, and by no means kill him; she is his mother."
>
> And all Israel heard of the judgment which the king had rendered; and they feared the king, for they saw that the wisdom of God was in him to administer justice.

Two harlots come before Solomon, both claiming that the child in question is theirs. The first accuses the second of switching babies after the second had accidentally killed her child while sleeping. Both women claim the child is theirs, and there are no other witnesses who come forward. Based on the claims, there is apparently no way for Solomon to decide who the real mother is based on evidence already available. It is very likely, though not recorded in Scripture, that this case had gone before other judges before coming to Solomon and they were not able to resolve the issue.

In the passage just before this account (1 Kings 3:5–15), Solomon asks God for "an understanding heart to judge Your people, that I may discern between good and evil." God is pleased with Solomon's request for discerning justice and grants his request.

In order to determine the identity of the true mother, Solomon calls for a sword and orders the child cut in half so that each woman may have a part of the child. The first woman compassionately — and likely very quickly — cries out (as most mothers would!), "O my lord, give her the living child, and by no means kill him!" This action exposes the true mother who would rather see her child alive and raised by another woman than cut in half. The jealousy and treachery of the second woman is exposed by her reply, "Let him be neither mine nor yours, but divide him."

Knowing that Solomon has been granted the ability to discern between good and evil in a just way, is it even reasonable to think that Solomon truly intended to cut the child in half? His call to action was a very wise way to expose the true mother based on her reaction to the peril of her child.

A Man of Many Wives

Roger Patterson

Does God condone polygamy?

> And he had seven hundred wives, princesses, and three hundred concubines; and his wives turned away his heart (1 Kings 11:3).

> A bishop then must be blameless, the husband of one wife, temperate, sober–minded, of good behavior, hospitable, able to teach (1 Timothy 3:2).

As we look at Scripture, it is clear that polygamous relationships are presented in the Bible. But does that mean that they are acceptable in God's eyes? We also see instances of lying, murder, and rape in the Bible, but these are clearly not acceptable. Just because the events are described does not mean they are condoned. There is no passage in the Bible that condones polygamy.

Beginning in Genesis, it is clear that God intended marriage to be between one woman and one man. Genesis 2 records the creation of one woman for Adam, and in verse 24 we see that because of this "a man shall leave his father and mother and be joined to his wife, and they shall become one flesh." If two makes one flesh, then three or more cannot also make one flesh. This is confirmed by Jesus in Matthew 19:3–9 as He is being questioned about divorce. Jesus quotes Genesis 2:24 as support for the idea of marriage being between one man and one woman "from the beginning." God's plan, from the beginning, was not for polygamous relationships.

As the Israelites were in the desert after the Exodus, God announces a prophecy through Moses. The Israelites will eventually call for a king to be set over them (Deuteronomy 17:14). Following that, God pronounces standards for the kings to come. In Deuteronomy 17:17 we see the command that the king shall not "multiply wives for himself, lest his heart turn away." God clearly commands that the king should not practice polygamy. So why would He condone its practice for anyone else?

Many Jewish leaders and patriarchs, including kings, were recorded to have polygamous relationships. However, these relationships brought about judgment and hardship. David was punished for his relationship with Bathsheba; Abraham's relationship with Hagar brought strife into the family; and other examples would also bear out this point. Some may argue that Jacob's polygamous lifestyle was blessed by God, but just because God used a sinful relationship to fulfill His plan does not mean that that action was right. Likewise, Jesus's lineage can be traced back to Bathsheba.

Polygamy was popular in many cultures, but that does not mean that it was right in God's eyes. Divorce was also allowed because of the hardness of the hearts of the Israelites (Matthew 19:8), but it was not part of God's "very good" creation. Jesus called the Jews of the day an "adulterous generation" who chose to live outside of God's rules and instead, made their own. Just because the Jews (or any other peoples) tolerated polygamy does not mean that God condoned it.

Two Ages at Once

Bodie Hodge and Stacia McKeever

How could Ahaziah be both 22 years old and 42 years old when he started to reign?

> Ahaziah was twenty-two years old when he became king, and he reigned one year in Jerusalem. His mother's name was Athaliah the granddaughter of Omri, king of Israel (2 Kings 8:26).

> Ahaziah was forty-two years old when he became king, and he reigned one year in Jerusalem. His mother's name was Athaliah the granddaughter of Omri (2 Chronicles 22:2).

Was Ahaziah 22 or 42 years old when he became king of Judah? Ahaziah's true age when he became king of Judah is easy to discern by further research. In 2 Kings 8:17, Ahaziah's father Joram reigned for 8 years after beginning his reign at age 32. Joram was 40 when he died, showing that Ahaziah could not have been 42, but was instead 22 when he began his reign. So what does the 42 in 2 Chronicles 22:2 indicate?

There are two primary answers that Christian scholars have given. Either answer reveals there is no contradiction:

> The 42 is in reference to the beginning of the kingly reign of which Ahaziah is a part.

> This was a copyist error that changed the original 22 in 2 Chronicles 22:2 to 42.

Was 42 Years the Beginning of the Kingly Reign?

Leading Hebraist Dr. John Gill listed several responses to this alleged contradiction in the 1700s:

> Some refer this to Jehoram, that he was forty two when Ahaziah began to reign, but he was but forty when he died. . . .

others to the age of Athaliah his mother, as if he was the son of one that was forty two, when he himself was but twenty two; but no instance is given of any such way of writing, nor any just reason for it. . . .

others make these forty two years reach to the twentieth of his son Joash, his age twenty two, his reign one, Athaliah six, and Joash thirteen. . . .

the one, that he was twenty two when he began to reign in his father's lifetime, and forty two when he began to reign in his own right; but then he must reign twenty years with his father, whereas his father reigned but eight years: to make this clear they observe, as Kimchi and Abarbinel, from whom this solution is taken, that he reigned eight years very happily when his son was twenty two, and taken on the throne with him, after which he reigned twenty more ingloriously, and died, when his son was forty two; this has been greedily received by many, but without any proof. . . .

that these forty two years are not the date of the age of Ahaziah, but of the reign of the family of Omri king of Israel; so the Jewish chronology; but how impertinent must the use of such a date be in the account of the reign of a king of Judah? All that can be said is, his mother was of that family, which is a trifling reason for such an unusual method of reckoning.[10]

Obviously, Dr. Gill was appealing for another view: that it was simply a copyist mistake. More recently, chronologist Dr. Floyd Jones expands on Gill's fifth explanation in *Chronology of the Old Testament* in much more detail.[11] This is a respectable position and is one of the two possibilities put forth by most scholars.

Dr. Jones makes the case that 42 should remain in 2 Chronicles 22:2. He points out that Ahaziah's age was indeed 22 as 2 Kings 8:26 says. However, he interprets 2 Chronicles 22:2 as the beginning of

---

10. Dr. John Gill, *Exposition of the Entire Bible*, commentary notes, 2 Chronicles 22:2, http://gill.biblecommenter.com.

11. Dr. Floyd Jones, *Chronology of the Old Testament* (Green Forest, AR: Master Books, 2005), p. 139–141.

the kingly reign of his family line (starting with Omri, then his son Ahab, and then Ahab's daughter Athaliah who was Ahaziah's wife).

Dr. Jones points out that the numbers given in the Hebrew text are not the numerals 42 and 22 but are written out as "two and forty" and "two and twenty," which would seem to make a copyist mistake less likely. Hence, he reinterprets the verse instead of appealing to a copyist mistake.

He points out that the words *was* and *old* in 2 Chronicles 22:2 are not in the original Hebrew but were added to the English translation to make it smoother. Without them, it reads "a son of 42 years." Dr. Jones states:

> Thus the sense of Ahaziah's being "a son of 42 years" in his reigning is seen to refer to his being a son of the dynasty of Omri which was in its 42nd year. Putting the two Scriptures together reveals that Ahaziah was 22 years old when he began to reign during the *42nd year of the dynasty of Omri*, of which he is also an integral part.[12]

Although this seems to answer this alleged contradiction, many are not entirely convinced. If 42 is to be interpreted as the beginning of the dynasty of Omri in 2 Chronicles, then why is 22 in 2 Kings 8 not also referring to the beginning of the dynasty of Omri? By this reasoning, this would mean the alleged contradiction could still exist. Another reason others are not entirely convinced is that other ancient texts have 22 in this verse, not 42. Let's look at the possibility of a copyist mistake.

Was It a Copyist Mistake?

Many fail to realize that several ancient texts have 22 (or simply 20) instead of 42 as listed in the Masoretic Text (MT) in 2 Chronicles 22:2. The Syriac version (common to Eastern churches) and Arabic version each have 22. The Septuagint (LXX) has 20. In fact, the version used by the Antioch church in New Testament times was obtained by Archbishop Ussher at great cost and it had 22 (see first reference by Gill in this alleged contradiction). These early

---

12. Ibid., p. 140, emphasis in original.

translations were obviously drawing from another Hebrew text, different from what we know today as the Masoretic or standard Hebrew text used for most translations in modern times.

So which text should be used in this instance? Before we assume the MT, let's see what Jesus quoted from. Jesus quoted from the Old Testament about 64 times in the Gospels. More than half of His quotes agree with both the LXX and the MT. In 12 instances, Jesus's quotes differ from both the LXX and the MT. In 7 instances, He sides with the LXX over the MT. And in another 12 instances, He agrees with the MT over the LXX. So if we make a case that other ancient texts such as the LXX should *never* be used instead of the MT, then Jesus would be in error as He clearly didn't draw explicitly from what we know today as the MT.[13]

Other ancient texts draw from Hebrew versions far earlier than the version of the MT that we have today (current extant copies date from A.D. 900 to 1000).[14] For example, the Septuagint was translated from Hebrew about 200 to 250 years before Christ. Our earliest copy of the Septuagint is from the A.D. 300s.[15] The Syriac version was probably done in the 1st century A.D. because of the rapid growth of the church in Antioch as recorded in the Book of Acts. It was surely completed by the 2nd century, which is commonly referenced.[16]

The Arabic version was done much later, in the 10th century by Saadia Gaon in Babylonia.[17] But this means it drew from a Hebrew text unique from the Masoretic to utilize 22 instead of 42 in 2 Chronicles 22:2. If this were a copyist mistake in the Masoretic text,

13. G. Miller, "Septuagint," *A Christian Thinktank*, http://www.christian-thinktank.com/alxx.html, January 30, 1995.

14. J. McDowell, *The New Evidence that Demand a Verdict* (Nashville, TN: Thomas Nelson, 1999), p. 77; J. McDowell, *A Ready Defense* (Nashville, TN: Thomas Nelson, 1993), p. 48.

15. B. Edwards, *Nothing But the Truth* (Darlington, UK: Evangelical Press, 2006), p. 248.

16. "Peshitta," *Wikipedia*, http://en.wikipedia.org/wiki/Peshitta, accessed December 15, 2008. There have been reports that the date is slightly later (3rd or 4th centuries) but it is still far earlier than A.D. 900.

17. "Saadia Gaon," *Jewish Virtual Library*, http://www.jewishvirtuallibrary.org/jsource/biography/SaadiaGaon.html, accessed December 15, 2008.

then it happened prior to the Masoretes who worked from the 7th to 11th centuries A.D., because Jerome's Latin Vulgate from A.D. 400 also has the number 42.

Regardless, all of these texts underwent some copyist mistakes, as they simply do not agree exactly with each other. This is why scholars such as Dr. Gill lean toward a copyist mistake. Consider what Dr. Gill says:

> Indeed it is more to the honour of the sacred Scriptures to acknowledge here and there a mistake in the copiers, especially in the historical books, where there is sometimes a strange difference of names and numbers, than to give in to wild and distorted interpretations of them, in order to reconcile them, where there is no danger with respect to any article of faith or manners.[18]

Other commentaries are also split on the subject. Had the 42 and 22 been written in *number* form prior to being spelled out, this discrepancy could easily creep in as *mem* (40) and *caph* (20) are very similar. We know for certain that as of about A.D. 900, the Masoretes have it spelled out (e.g., "two and forty" or "two and twenty").

The point is that copies and translations are not inerrant (this is different from preservation). Recognizing this gives more credit to God's originals and focuses less on the fallible copyists since. Also, it stresses the need to handle the copies and translations of the Word of God with great care and reverence. Had translations and copies been kept inerrant, which Scripture doesn't reveal, then they should all be identical and yet they are not. God has preserved His Word in a variety of copies and has warned against changing His Word. For example, Revelation 22:18–19 reveals that a horrible fate awaits those who changed words when copying the Book of Revelation.

Regardless, either explanation (42 being the beginning of Ahaziah's kingly family line or a copyist mistake) reduces this alleged discrepancy to nothing and neither harm the integrity of the original inerrant Bible manuscripts.

---

18. Dr. John Gill, *Exposition of the Entire Bible*, commentary notes, 2 Chronicles 22:2, http://gill.biblecommenter.com.

Postscript: A Note on Preservation

The Masoretic text is easily the best collection of Hebrew manuscripts of the Old Testament; however, we need to keep in mind that it, too, is a copy of a copy of a copy, etc. And copyists were never given the privilege of inerrancy, unlike the prophets or Apostles. Although the MT may be the best, we need to be careful about in-depth studies of words and phrases without consulting other ancient texts.

This brings us to the question of "preservation," which is distinct from inerrancy. God reveals that He would preserve His Word (Psalm 12:6–7). Currently there are two views on how this preservation has taken place:

> One preserved inerrant copy of a copy of a copy (etc.) has been passed down.
>
> Preservation has occurred through the various copies that exist.

Throughout the history of the Church, the second view has been dominant. With English translations, for example, from Tyndale forward, each translator made use of textually criticized texts and often consulted variant texts when doing translations. This shouldn't come as a surprise. The idea that *one inerrant copy lineage* has been passed along is a relatively new idea that, sadly, doesn't take into account the past.[19]

Early English translators relied heavily on the various Textus Receptus (TR) editions, published copies of the Greek New Testament, as well as a few other sources, whether English, Latin, or other. Dutch Catholic Erasmus in 1516 did textual criticism of a handful of variant copies (three primary copies and three others) of the Greek New Testament to arrive at this new text.[20] He even used quotations by church fathers for comparison and back-translated

---

19. For a more detailed history of the Bible in English please see Donald Brake, *A Visual History of the English Bible* (Grand Rapids, MI: Baker Books, 2008).

20. Erasmus 1516, *Bibliography of Textual Criticism*, http://www.bible-researcher.com/bib-e.html, accessed December 15, 2008.

excerpts of Revelation from the Latin Vulgate that did not appear in any versions of his Greek copies.

Erasmus issued three editions of his Greek New Testament, the latter editions correcting earlier errors. His first edition was apparently rushed for competition with another family of texts that was used for the Polyglot Bible, and it became the dominant text used throughout Europe. Others, such as Stephanus, Beza, and the Elzevir brothers, further edited Erasmus's TR for subsequent printings. So early translations such as Tyndale's, the Geneva Bible, Luther's Bible, and other New Testaments generally came from this text family because this was what was available. But even then, popular versions such as the King James New Testament differs from the TR nearly 170 times and over 60 times agreed with the Latin Vulgate over *any* Greek text, including the TR.[21]

Since the time of Erasmus, nearly 5,300 Greek texts and fragments have been found.[22] So why remain confined to Erasmus's small library that didn't even have a complete version of Revelation in Greek? There have been many attempts to utilize these other texts instead of ignore them. Among the most popular was Westcott and Hort's text. But as far as we know, no modern translation uses the Westcott and Hort text except the poorly translated New World Translation.[23]

There has been further study and textual criticism to arrive at standard texts. Today, the latest editions are used when translating the Bible, whether Old Testament or New Testament. The Lord has preserved other texts besides the MT so that we're able to compare various texts. Truly, He has preserved His Word.

---

21. Douglas Kutilek, "Westcott and Hort vs. Textus Receptus: Which Is Superior?" May 24, 1996, reprinted at http://www.bible-researcher.com/kutilek1.html, accessed December 15, 2008.

22. J. McDowell, *A Ready Defense* (Nashville, TN: Thomas Nelson Publishers, 1993), p. 43.

23. *New World Translation of the Holy Scriptures (Revised)* (Brooklyn, NY: Watchtower Bible and Tract Society of Pennsylvania and the International Bible Students Association, 1984), p. 5.

Get Out of Jail Twice

Bodie Hodge

Was Jehoiachin set free from prison on 25th day (Jeremiah 52:31) of the month or the 27th day of the month (2 Kings 25:27)?

The relevant passages are:

> Now it came to pass in the thirty-seventh year of the captivity of Jehoiachin king of Judah, in the twelfth month, on the twenty-fifth day of the month, that Evil-Merodach king of Babylon, in the first year of his reign, lifted up the head of Jehoiachin king of Judah and brought him out of prison (Jeremiah 52:31).

> Now it came to pass in the thirty-seventh year of the captivity of Jehoiachin king of Judah, in the twelfth month, on the twenty-seventh day of the month, that Evil-Merodach king of Babylon, in the year that he began to reign, released Jehoiachin king of Judah from prison (2 Kings 25:27).

Many Christians assume that this alleged discrepancy is a "copyist mistake" because it involves numbers. Numbers would be, after all, a reasonable mistake when copying from another manuscript. In fact, if one were to search books or the Internet on this alleged contradiction, the likely answer given by Christians is that this is a copyist mistake.

However, before one assumes this, I suggest we take a closer look at what these two verses are saying. In both verses, the passages have some portions that are identical and others that are not; the form is below:

> Now it came to pass in the thirty-seventh year of the captivity of Jehoiachin king of Judah, in the twelfth month [date] that

Evil-Merodach king of Babylon, in the first year of his reign . . . [further information].

This would be a legitimate contradiction, or perhaps a copyist mistake, if the date were different, but the further information was identical. But this is not the case and, accordingly, the further information proves very significant in this case. So let's take a closer look at this further information.

Jeremiah 52:31 has that on the date of the 25th the king of Babylon "lifted up the head of Jehoiachin king of Judah and brought him out of prison." On the other hand, 2 Kings 25:27 has that on the date of the 27th the king of Babylon "released Jehoiachin king of Judah from prison."

These are two different dates, indeed, because they are referring to two different instances. On the 25th, the king of Babylon gives the decree to release Jehoiachin king of Judah. But it took a couple of days for Jehoiachin king of Judah to actually be released.

Hence, this is no contradiction; rather, the Bible is actually being much more specific in the details than the reader may first realize. Even in today's culture, if a prisoner is pardoned by a governing official like the president, it takes time before the person is released from prison — the orders need to be verified, paperwork filed, etc. So two days is not unreasonable.

This should be a lesson to Christians, too. When an alleged contradiction is brought to our attention, the first place we should look is the Scriptures themselves, and then think logically about the verses in question.

Mixed Prophets

Paul F. Taylor and Bodie Hodge

Did Matthew (27:9) falsely attribute a prophecy to Jeremiah that came from Zechariah (11:12–13)?

Many skeptics and liberal scholars have suggested that Matthew's gospel contains an error:

> Then was fulfilled what was spoken by Jeremiah the prophet, saying, "And they took the thirty pieces of silver, the value of Him who was priced, whom they of the children of Israel priced, and gave them for the potter's field, as the LORD directed me" (Matthew 27:9–10).

The quotation about the 30 pieces of silver is highly reminiscent of Zechariah, and it is therefore assumed that Matthew made a mistake. If Matthew did make a mistake, then the concept of scriptural inerrancy is undermined.

The most significant error that the skeptics make is to approach this passage deliberately looking for an error. If we look at the passage, while assuming scriptural inerrancy, we can see that there are several rationalizations of the alleged problem that have been discussed over the years. In short they are:

1. Said by Jeremiah but later written by Zechariah.

2. Zechariah's second name is Jeremiah, like "Simon Peter" for Peter.

3. Copyist mistake, but the Syriac and Persian versions have no prophet listed and all the Greek versions do.

4. This is quoting from an apocryphal work of Jeremiah, like Jude quoting from Enoch.

5. The last four chapters of Zechariah were actually written by Jeremiah.

6. Due to a different order of books in the Jewish canon, Jeremiah could be given proper credit for any of the minor prophets.

7. This passage refers to both sections of Jeremiah and Zechariah, and only Jeremiah is mentioned.

The first five are less likely, with the last two being the more common explanations (6 and 7). Let's take a closer look at them.

A Collection of Prophetic Books (6)

This possibility is that Matthew is using a well-established rabbinical formula of referring to a collection of books by the name of the first book in the collection. Jesus used a similar formula in Luke 24:44, where He referred to the Writings section of the Old Testament as Psalms — even though this could include the other writings, such as Proverbs.

In the Jewish Tanakh, the prophetic books were in a different order then the order of the Christian Bible — even though they are all there. The first listed book in the collection of the Prophets was Jeremiah, not Isaiah. Therefore, a citation of Jeremiah could conceivably cover an actual quotation from Zechariah.

The Context of Jeremiah (7)

This explanation involves the way that New Testament writers frequently allude to more than one Old Testament passage, providing an overall context. For the quote by Zechariah, there is a lot of foundational information that is necessary. First, Jeremiah 18 is the famous portion of the Old Testament that discusses God being the Potter and we the clay. And the Lord warns of a disaster to a nation that turns to evil. Israel had just rejected the Son of God, and the spiritual leaders just purchased His death for 30 pieces of silver. The message of the gospel then also went out to the Gentiles. And Israel, particularly Jerusalem, was soon left in ruin.

Also, Jeremiah 19:1–4 gives a more precise placement of the potter's field, outside the Potsherd Gate of Jerusalem, and the catastrophe that will happen there. The verse mentions that Israel has forsaken God here, and mentions the blood of innocents there too — Christ's even being the ultimate innocent blood.

Then, of course, Jeremiah 32:9–12 discusses the land and purchase agreements. Although the first quotation in Matthew 27:9–10 is somewhat similar to the passage in Zechariah, the second quotation — "and gave them for the potter's field, as the LORD directed me" — alludes to Jeremiah 32:6–9, which refers to the potter's field.

So these three aspects are Jeremiah's, and Zechariah seems to build on them. In that respect, it is not an error to refer to the prophet Jeremiah at the point.

Another Possible Explanation (8)

If we look carefully at these two verses in Matthew and Zechariah, though they have similarities, they simply do not match up:

> Then I said to them, "If it is agreeable to you, give me my wages; and if not, refrain." So they weighed out for my wages thirty pieces of silver. And the LORD said to me, "Throw it to the potter" — that princely price they set on me. So I took the thirty pieces of silver and threw them into the house of the LORD for the potter (Zechariah 11:12–13).

> Then was fulfilled what was spoken by Jeremiah the prophet, saying, "And they took the thirty pieces of silver, the value of Him who was priced, whom they of the children of Israel priced, and gave them for the potter's field, as the LORD directed me" (Matthew 27:9–10).

One quote says that they "weighed out" the wages, the other says "and they took." One says "throw it to the potter," and this was already fulfilled in Matthew 27:5. One does not mention that it was for a potter's field, and one does. One could find other differences, but this should suffice. The point it, this is not a quote from the Book of Zechariah.

One cannot say this quote was misattributed to Zechariah, since Zechariah said no such thing — his quote had a few similar aspects, but that is as far as it should go. So if Matthew, speaking with the Holy Spirit, quotes this and attributes it to Jeremiah, then it was indeed something Jeremiah said, and it was merely not recorded in his writings. Recall John speaking about Jesus:

> And there are also many other things that Jesus did, which if they were written one by one, I suppose that even the world itself could not contain the books that would be written. Amen (John 21:25).

So the answer could be as simple as this quote by Matthew is not by Zechariah but is merely an unrecorded quote by Jeremiah. Note also that Matthew does not say that the quotation was *written* by Jeremiah, but rather *spoken* (*rheo*) by Jeremiah. It is possible, therefore, that the Holy Spirit inspired Matthew to report a spoken prophecy of Jeremiah, just as Jude was inspired to include previously unwritten information about Michael in his book (Jude 9). After the spoken prophecy given to Jeremiah, the Holy Spirit could later have inspired a similar prophecy to Zechariah as part of his *written* account.

Regardless, there are eight possible explanations given for this, and these last three easily answer the alleged contradiction.

Sleeping in the Temple

Paul F. Taylor

How could the young Samuel have been sleeping in the temple when the temple was not built until much later?

There are two allegations referred to 1 Samuel 3:3. The verse is quoted below from the KJV, the NIV, and the NKJV.

And ere the lamp of God went out in the temple of the LORD, where the ark of God was, and Samuel was laid down to sleep (KJV).

The lamp of God had not yet gone out, and Samuel was lying down in the temple of the LORD, where the ark of God was (NIV).

Before the lamp of God went out in the tabernacle of the LORD where the ark of God was, and while Samuel was lying down (NKJV).

The translation used by the NKJV gives a clue as to where the first misunderstanding comes from. The Hebrew word is *hekäl*. This word is used of the temple, but the meaning of the word is literally a large building or edifice. Commentators[24] have suggested that before the building of the temple the word was often applied to the sacred tabernacle. Therefore, it is perfectly possible for Samuel to have been asleep in this tabernacle. This alleged discrepancy is not so much a mistranslation as a misunderstanding.

The other alleged discrepancy with this verse is that Samuel was sleeping in the sacred portion of this tabernacle, the holy of holies, where the ark of God was. The NKJV gets it correct by pointing out that light went out where the holy of holies was while Samuel was lying down, not that he was lying down in this very holy place. This shows the difficulty of translating Hebrew into English when not careful.

24. See, for example, John Haley, *Alleged Discrepancies of the Bible* (New Kensington, PA, Whitaker House, 2004), p. 396.

As Easy as Pi

Dr. Jason Lisle

Does the Bible make a mistake in claiming that pi equals 3?

It has been alleged that the Bible is in error because it teaches that pi is equal to 3. Recall that pi is the ratio of circumference to diameter in a circle. And even most young students know that pi is not exactly equal to three. It is often approximated as 3.14, though the actual decimal expansion goes on forever: 3.141592653589793. . . . It is not difficult to measure the diameter and circumference of a circle to confirm that pi does indeed have this value. So is the Bible in error?

The relevant passage is 1 Kings 7:23, which states:

> Now he made the sea of cast metal ten cubits from brim to brim, circular in form, and its height was five cubits, and thirty cubits in circumference (NASB).

This verse describes a cylindrical vessel built at the order of Solomon. First of all, notice that this passage does *not* say "*exactly* ten cubits" or "*exactly* thirty cubits." The numbers have been rounded to the nearest integer (or possibly the nearest multiple of ten). Dividing the circumference (30 cubits) by the diameter (10 cubits), we infer that pi is approximately equal to three. But of course, pi *is* approximately equal to three, so the passage is quite correct.

At best, critics of the Bible could say that the Bible is *imprecise* here, but they cannot legitimately say that it is *inaccurate* or *mistaken*. Even scientists today will round off numbers at appropriate times. Remember that any decimal expression of pi must be rounded at some point anyway, since the expansion is infinite. There is no fallacy in rounding a number.

Second, we should consider the matter of significant figures. On a physics test, if a circle is said to have a diameter of 10 feet and the student is asked to compute the circumference, the correct answer is 30 feet — *not* 31 feet. The reason 31 feet is an incorrect answer is because it implies a precision that is unwarranted by the given information. The value 10 feet indicates that the diameter has been rounded. Perhaps it has been rounded up from the exact value of 9.5 feet, in which case the exact diameter would be 29.845 . . . feet — which rounds up to 30 feet.

Third, we should consider 1 Kings 7:26, which states that this cylindrical vessel "was a handbreadth thick." Since the diameter is given from "brim to brim" (verse 23), the 10 cubits is referring to the outer diameter (which includes the handbreadth thickness of the rim). However, the circumference may well refer to the inner circle (as this is more representative of the pool of water inside the cylinder), which excludes the handbreadth. So even if we take the outer diameter to be exactly 10 cubits, the inner diameter would be smaller. A handbreadth is roughly 1/4 of a cubit; so, the inner diameter would be 10 cubits — (0.25 x 2) cubits = 9.50 cubits. This means the inner circumference would be 29.845 . . . cubits, which rounds up to 30 cubits (*not* 31 cubits).

In conclusion, the accusation that the Bible has made a mathematical mistake is totally without merit. The biblical answer is spot on, given the information presented and the precision of the numbers in question.

Matthew – John

Problems with Basic Math?

Bodie Hodge

Was Matthew incapable of basic math in his genealogy?

Matthew's genealogy of Jesus says there were three groups of 14 people from Abraham to Christ, but when you add them up, there are only 41 people, not the expected 42. How do you explain that?

When we turn to Matthew 1, we read:

> So all the generations from Abraham to David are fourteen generations, from David until the captivity in Babylon are fourteen generations, and from the captivity in Babylon until the Christ are fourteen generations (Matthew 1:17).

Just prior to this, we read genealogical data that is tallied up in the following chart:

Verse	Father	Son	Number
Abraham			
2	Abraham	Isaac	1
2	Isaac	Jacob (Israel)	2
2	Jacob (Israel)	Judah	3
3	Judah	Perez	4
3	Perez	Hezron	5
3	Hezron	Ram	6
4	Ram	Amminadab	7
4	Amminadab	Nahshon	8
4	Nahshon	Salmon	9
5	Salmon	Boaz	10
5	Boaz	Obed	11

Demolishing Contradictions

Verse	Father	Son	Number
5	Obed	Jesse	12
	David		
6	David	Solomon	1
7	Solomon	Rehoboam	2
7	Rehoboam	Abijah	3
7	Abijah	Asa	4
8	Asa	Jehoshaphat	5
8	Jehoshaphat	Joram	6
8	Joram	Uzziah	7
9	Uzziah	Jotham	8
9	Jotham	Ahaz	9
9	Ahaz	Hezekiah	10
10	Hezekiah	Manasseh	11
10	Manasseh	Amon	12
10	Amon	Josiah	13
	Jeconiah (Jehoiachin)		
12	Jeconiah	Shealtiel	1
12	Shealtiel	Zerubbabel	2
13	Zerubbabel	Abihud	3
13	Abihud	Eliakim	4
13	Eliakim	Azor	5
14	Azor	Zadok	6
14	Zadok	Achim	7
14	Achim	Eliud	8
15	Eliud	Eleazar	9
15	Eleazar	Matthan	10
15	Matthan	Jacob	11
16	Jacob	Joseph	12
16	Joseph	Whose wife, Mary, bore Jesus	13

In Matthew 1:17, we find this was specifically broken down into three major divisions:

- Abraham to David
- From David to the captivity
- From the captivity to the Messiah

The verse also reveals that the divisions will be groups of 14, not complete genealogies like Luke 3. But what about the 14 generations here. Isn't there a contradiction, since some don't reveal exactly 14 generations each? Take care in noticing how these names and divisions are given, and the answer presents itself.

The first division is "from Abraham to David." So this would include both David and Abraham and the 12 generations listed between them to make 14.

The second division is "from David to the deportation." So this *includes* David again in the count, but not necessarily Jeconiah; otherwise, it would have made sense to use his name. The Jewish community would have been very familiar with Jeconiah and his relation to the deportation. But Jeconiah is not listed here by name; rather, *the deportation* is named. This is a significant point.

Jeconiah was only king for a short time, recorded as doing evil, and was young, being only 18 when he took the crown (2 Chronicles 36:9). So, there is no reason to assume that Matthew included Jeconiah as a full *generation* (which is what Matthew is writing about). So from David to the deportation (not including Jeconiah), there are 14 generations.

The final division is "from the deportation to the Messiah." Since Jeconiah was not listed with the previous division at the deportation, he will no doubt be included here, since the time of his generation was more complete *after* the deportation. When adding the generations, from Jeconiah to Christ, there are 14 generations.

So Matthew was entirely accurate with his wording of each of the 14 generations. Using Matthew's breakdown, David was listed twice, hence no contradiction, but careful wording on Matthew's part.

Seeds of Dissent

Stacia McKeever

Was Jesus wrong in Matthew 13:31–32 when He said that the mustard seed was the "least of all the seeds"?

> Another parable He put forth to them, saying: "The kingdom of heaven is like a mustard seed, which a man took and sowed in his field, which indeed is the least of all the seeds; but when it is grown it is greater than the herbs and becomes a tree, so that the birds of the air come and nest in its branches" (Matthew 13:31–32).

Skeptics claim that Jesus was wrong in saying that the mustard seed was the least of all the seeds, or that He was accommodating the knowledge of His listeners. The late Professor of New Testament Language and Literature W. Harold Mare covered this topic more than adequately when he responded to the critics in a paper published in the *Grace Theological Journal* (which was published by Grace Theological Seminary from 1960–1991). In it, he says:

> Jesus' statement in Matthew 13:32 about the size of the mustard seed need not, and has no reason to, be interpreted as contradictory to scientific evidence for the following reasons.

> In the first place, although, the orchid seed may be the smallest, or one of the smallest plant seeds, and thus smaller than the mustard seed, it is not necessary to consider Jesus' statement in Matthew 13:32 as containing scientific error since the class of seeds with which the mustard seed is associated is the garden herb group (lachana) which may possibly be interpreted as being the "all the seeds" category to which reference is made in the earlier part of the statement, "all" there being limited to the specific group (lachana) under consideration in the total context of the verse. Since the mustard seed probably was cultivated in Palestine in ancient times, for its oil,

it may be argued that Jesus, when speaking of this type of seed, was talking about it in a comparison with all those seeds which were planted by farmers for food. Since panton is used with the lachana group in the parallel passage in Mark 4:31, it may be further argued that the panton ton spermaton group in both Matthew 13:32 and Mark 4:31 is intended to mean only the lachana species, the "all the garden herb" group. In this limited context of garden herbs then, Jesus speaks of the mustard seed as extremely small.

With "all the seeds" being understood as limited in this way by the context, the minute orchid seed need not be considered as being included by Jesus in His statement. It is to be observed that if Jesus had said, "The mustard seed is smaller than the orchid seed," He would have seemed to have spoken erroneously; but this He did not say.

Secondly, that the expression comparing smallness with the size of mustard seed was a common Jewish saying argues for the fact that scientific literalness and preciseness need not be pressed upon it, it being able to be understood then, as men certainly understand it now, as a general and popular expression of smallness.

However, it is to be realized that Jesus, in using the common Jewish proverbial expression of the mustard seed as a figure of smallness, did so only because the proverbial expression so used was a true and accurate statement, including those implications involving scientific data regarding the mustard seed, both as to its very smallness as a seed and to its moderate largeness when grown.[25]

---

25. W. Harold Mare, "The Smallest Mustard Seed — Matthew 13:32," *Grace Theological Journal* 9.3 (1968): 3–11; online here: http://faculty.gordon.edu/hu/bi/ted_hildebrandt/ NTeSources/NTArticles/GTJ-NT/Mare-MatMustard-GTJ-68.htm.

Against the Law

Roger Patterson

Doesn't Jesus contradict Old Testament teachings by not stoning the adulteress, which was commanded?

Relevant passages besides the Ten Commandments that forbid adultery (Exodus 20:14; Deuteronomy 5:18) are:

> The man who commits adultery with another man's wife, he who commits adultery with his neighbor's wife, the adulterer and the adulteress, shall surely be put to death (Leviticus 20:10).

> Then the scribes and Pharisees brought to Him a woman caught in adultery. And when they had set her in the midst, they said to Him, "Teacher, this woman was caught in adultery, in the very act. Now Moses, in the law, commanded us that such should be stoned. But what do You say?"

> This they said, testing Him, that they might have something of which to accuse Him. But Jesus stooped down and wrote on the ground with His finger, as though He did not hear. So when they continued asking Him, He raised Himself up and said to them, "He who is without sin among you, let him throw a stone at her first." And again He stooped down and wrote on the ground.

> Then those who heard it, being convicted by their conscience, went out one by one, beginning with the oldest even to the last. And Jesus was left alone, and the woman standing in the midst. When Jesus had raised Himself up and saw no one but the woman, He said to her, "Woman, where are those accusers of yours? Has no one condemned you?"

> She said, "No one, Lord." And Jesus said to her, "Neither do I condemn you; go and sin no more" (John 8:3–11).

> Whoever is deserving of death shall be put to death on the testimony of two or three witnesses; he shall not be put to death on the testimony of one witness (Deuteronomy 17:6).

One witness shall not rise against a man concerning any iniquity or any sin that he commits; by the mouth of two or three witnesses the matter shall be established (Deuteronomy 19:15).

In the passage referred to, a woman is brought to Jesus by the religious leaders who were interested in trapping Him in a difficult situation. Many apparent witnesses have been found to condemn this woman who has been caught in the very act of adultery. According to the laws given to Moses and laid out in Exodus, Leviticus, and Deuteronomy, adultery was a sin punishable by death — for the man and the woman! It is interesting to note that only the woman was brought before Jesus. This exposes the motives of the religious leaders. They were not interested in justice, but in accusing Jesus so they might discredit His authority.

One of the requirements of the administration of justice laid out in the Mosaic Law was that there must be agreement between two or three witnesses (Deuteronomy 17:6, 19:15) to condemn the accused. Jesus also faced this same standard in the trial that was held before Caiaphas (Matthew 26:57–60). When the witnesses were not in agreement, they were dismissed until two that were in agreement could be found.

After the leaders present the accused woman to Jesus, He stoops and writes something on the ground, ignoring the leaders. Though Scripture does not record what He wrote, some have speculated it was the Ten Commandments. Regardless, the leaders were convicted of their own sinfulness when Jesus asked those who were without sin to cast the first stone. As they walk away one by one, the woman is left standing alone. With no witnesses to accuse her, Jesus is justified in letting her go. He is not violating the Mosaic Law referenced by the Jewish leaders as there are no witnesses to provide testimony to condemn her.

Jesus exercises grace in His treatment of the woman without violating the letter of the Law. As God in the flesh, Jesus also has the authority to forgive sins (Matthew 9:6). It is clear from the text and a proper understanding of the application of Mosaic Law that the contradiction is apparent, and not real.

Counting Offspring

Stacia McKeever

If Jesus is God's "only begotten Son," then how can angels and Christians also be God's sons?

It is clear from verses such as the following that one title for Jesus is "Son of God."

> And suddenly they cried out, saying, "What have we to do with You, Jesus, You Son of God? Have You come here to torment us before the time?" (Matthew 8:29).

> Then those who were in the boat came and worshiped Him, saying, "Truly You are the Son of God" (Matthew 14:33).

> And the high priest arose and said to Him, "Do You answer nothing? What is it these men testify against You?" But Jesus kept silent. And the high priest answered and said to Him, "I put You under oath by the living God: Tell us if You are the Christ, the Son of God!" Jesus said to him, "It is as you said. Nevertheless, I say to you, hereafter you will see the Son of Man sitting at the right hand of the Power, and coming on the clouds of heaven" (Matthew 26:62–64).

> The beginning of the gospel of Jesus Christ, the Son of God (Mark 1:1).

Throughout Scripture, others are also called "son(s) of God."

- Adam (Luke 3:38)
- Angels (Job 1:6, 2:1, 38:7)
- Believers (Matthew 5:9; Romans 8:14, 19; Galatians 3:26)

"A son of God" or "sons of God" are monikers for those who follow after God. But the phrase "the Son of God" is used only for Jesus Christ. He is called the "only begotten Son" to be more precise (John 1:14, 3:16, 3:18; 1 John 4:9) and "His [God's] own Son"

(Romans 8:3). Jesus is referred to as "the Son" when God is referred to as "the Father" (John 3:35–36, 5:19–27, 6:40, 17:1; 2 John 1:9; Matthew 28:19). In fact, Jesus is the Son, the second person of the godhead, which cannot be said of any human or angel.

When understood from the whole context of Scripture, there is really no contradiction. Jesus is called "the only begotten" as the unique Son of God in a very real sense that no angelic being or member of humanity can share.

A Staff or Not?

Stacia McKeever

Did Jesus tell His disciples to take a staff?

These twelve Jesus sent out and commanded them, saying: "Do not go into the way of the Gentiles, and do not enter a city of the Samaritans. But go rather to the lost sheep of the house of Israel. And as you go, preach, saying, 'The kingdom of heaven is at hand.' Heal the sick, cleanse the lepers, raise the dead, cast out demons. Freely you have received, freely give. Provide neither gold nor silver nor copper in your money belts, nor bag for your journey, nor two tunics, nor sandals, nor staffs; for a worker is worthy of his food" (Matthew 10:5–10).

He commanded them to take nothing for the journey except a staff — no bag, no bread, no copper in their money belts — but to wear sandals, and not to put on two tunics (Mark 6:8–9).

Then He called His twelve disciples together and gave them power and authority over all demons, and to cure diseases. He sent them to preach the kingdom of God and to heal the sick. And He said to them, "Take nothing for the journey, neither staffs nor bag nor bread nor money; and do not have two tunics apiece" (Luke 9:1–3).

In these parallel passages, Jesus issues an urgent command to His 12 students — go and preach the immediacy of the kingdom of heaven to your Jewish brethren. Our English translations contain an apparent discrepancy in what Jesus told them to take with them — were they to take a staff or not? The issue can be cleared up studying the Greek words used for provide or take in the original manuscripts.

The sense of Matthew's "provide" (*ktaomai*) is "to get or acquire." In this passage, Jesus seems to urge His disciples to go now, don't take the time to find another staff, just take what you have and go. He promised that the disciples would be provided for, so they didn't need to make elaborate preparation.

Mark uses a word with a broader meaning (*airo*), which indicates "lift or take up." In this passage, Mark seems to convey the idea that Jesus wanted the disciples to take what they already have and go. Those who already had a staff were to take it but were not to acquire another staff. In the same vein, they should wear the sandals they had on but weren't to find an additional pair. They were to wear the tunic they already had on but weren't to get another.

Although using the same word for "take" as Mark, Luke's passage conveys the same sense as Matthew's. (Some scholars suggest that Luke probably gained his information mostly from Matthew's book and didn't have access to the book written by Mark.) Luke also conveys the idea that the disciples were to depart quickly and without taking lots of "things" with them. They needed to focus on preaching the kingdom of heaven and were to trust the Lord to provide for their needs.

What's in a Father's Name?

Bodie Hodge

Why does Joseph (Jesus's supposed father) have two different fathers listed in Matthew 1:16 and Luke 3:23?

> And Jacob begot Joseph the husband of Mary, of whom was born Jesus who is called Christ (Matthew 1:16).

> Now Jesus Himself began His ministry at about thirty years of age, being (as was supposed) the son of Joseph, the son of Heli (Luke 3:23).

First, a few preliminary comments need to be addressed. Luke's genealogy is complete, and Matthew's is merely a selected one. Matthew's genealogy was not meant to be complete according to Matthew 1:17, where it is specifically broken into groups of 14.

The two genealogies trace through two of David's sons, and both trace to Abraham. Matthew focuses on the kingly relationship through David and ultimately to the Jewish patriarch Abraham. However, Luke doesn't stop there. He continues to trace Christ's genealogy back to Adam. Luke focuses more on the humanity of Christ going back to Adam, where sin and death first entered into creation — hence the need for a Savior in the first place.

Another note is that both genealogies are aware of Mary's virgin birth. For example Matthew says: "Joseph the husband of Mary, of whom (feminine) was born Jesus." Luke is more obvious in that he says: "being (as was supposed) the son of Joseph."

With regard to the alleged "two fathers" of Joseph, the explanation of the differences between Matthew 1 and Luke 3 is quite simple. Luke traced Christ's lineage through Mary, while Matthew traced it through Joseph.[26]

Matthew's Genealogy

One of the main reasons Matthew is recording Joseph's lineage is due to Jeconiah (variant spellings: Jechonias, Jehoiakim). He is listed in Matthew 1:11. Because of Jeconiah's actions, a prophecy came down from God that none of his descendants would ever sit on the throne of David. Jesus, who forever sits on this throne, could not have been a physical descendant of Jeconiah (Jeremiah 22:30). A virgin birth would obviously prevent this.

This indicates that Matthew's genealogy is Joseph's, and this confirms the significance of the feminine verbiage. When Matthew mentioned Joseph's wife, Mary, at the end of the genealogical list, he used the feminine form for the parent of Jesus. This reveals that Jesus was indeed Mary's son and not Joseph's.

Luke's Genealogy

When looking at Luke 3, the genealogical list is strictly men from Jesus to Adam, whereas in Matthew's list, some women were included, such as Tamar, Ruth, and so on. So if this were a genealogy of Mary, then she would be listed.

Moreover, in the genealogy, Heli is listed as the father of Joseph, who had two daughters. The first is Mary, and the other was Zebedee's unnamed wife (Matthew 27:56; John 19:25). When there were no sons to preserve the inheritance in accordance with the Law of Moses (Numbers 27:1–11, 36:1–12), the husband would become the son upon marriage to keep up the family name. Therefore, Joseph, when he married Mary, became the son of Heli according to the Law of Moses and could legally be included in the genealogy.

Also, in Luke's genealogy the form is different from that of Matthew's. Matthew's list gives the father and who they begot (Greek

---

26. Evangelicals have pointed out other explanations for this alleged contradiction. But for the sake of brevity, we went with the most common satisfactory explanation.

gennao). In Luke, the form is different, where X is the son of Y. But more precisely, the word *son* is absent in Greek, but only inserted into English so we can better understand it. The only place where *son* is used in the Greek is in verse 23 where Jesus was the supposed son of Joseph, of Heli, of Matthat, of Levi, and so on.

Luke is being very precise. Jesus was thought to be the son of Joseph, who was *of* Heli. Notice that Luke never said that Joseph was the son of Heli in the Greek. This reduces the alleged contradiction to nothing and shows that Luke's genealogy is Mary's — with Joseph's name listed due to inheritance laws — and Matthew's genealogy is Joseph's.

Greater Than or Equal To

Paul F. Taylor and Bodie Hodge

If Jesus is God (John 1; Colossians 1; Hebrews 1; Philippians 2:5–8), then why was the Father greater than Jesus in John 14:28?

> "You have heard Me say to you, 'I am going away and coming back to you.' If you loved Me, you would rejoice because I said, 'I am going to the Father,' for My Father is greater than I" (John 14:28).

We have discussed the doctrine of the Trinity in a number of places on the AiG website.[27] A corollary is that the Father is God, Jesus is God, and the Spirit is God — one God in three persons. A number of passages emphasize that Jesus is God (e.g., Philippians 2:5–8). Some people have stumbled over the phrase "being in the form of God," as if this phrase implies a relationship that is less than equal. Actually, in the Greek, this phrase is even stronger than just saying, "Jesus is God." The phrase is closer to saying, "Jesus manifests God." The phrase states that Jesus and the Father are one in essence. Of course, John 1:1–3 points out that Jesus, the Word, created all things and so on.

Having accepted the deity of Christ, what are we to make of Jesus' statement in John 14:28 that "My Father is greater than I"? Pseudo-Christian religions make much of this verse. For example, a Jehovah's Witnesses publication called *What Does God Require of Us?* references this verse to "prove" that Jesus is inferior to God.[28]

---

27. http://www.answersingenesis.org/get-answers/v/recent/k/trinity.

28. "What Does God Require of Us?" (Watch Tower Bible and Tract Society of Pennsylvania, 2006), section 11.

The misunderstanding here arises by confusing Christ's divine nature with His human nature. Jesus is both fully human and fully God. J.C. Ryle puts it this way: "Trinitarians maintain the humanity of Christ as strongly as His divinity. . . . While Christ as God is equal to the Father, as man He is inferior to the Father."[29] Calvin puts it similarly: "Christ does not now speak either of his human nature, or of his eternal Divinity, but, accommodating himself to our weakness, places himself between God and us."[30]

This ties in with the Philippians passage in which we read that Jesus "made Himself of no reputation, taking the form of a bondservant, and coming in the likeness of men" (Philippians 2:7). Simply put, in His humanity, Christ is lesser than God the Father. But in His deity, He is equal. This explains why Mark 13:32 says that even the Son didn't know something the Father did. As soon as we understand Christ's dual nature, the alleged contradiction disappears.

In fact, this is the only way any of us can make any sense at all of the biblical language. On the one hand, there are distinct functions in the work of redemption voluntarily assumed by each member of the godhead and expressed in language of deference and submission. On the other hand, there is perfect equality — each divine person sharing the same divine essence in an inter-trinitarian relationship.

29. J.C. Ryle, *Expository Thoughts on John*, vol. 3, (Edinburgh: Banner of Truth, 1987 edition), p. 102.

30. See Calvin's complete commentary on John 14:25–28.

Crossed Messages

Dr. Georgia Purdom

Why do the inscriptions on Jesus' Cross differ among the four gospels?

The relevant passages are:

> And they put up over His head the accusation written against Him: THIS IS JESUS THE KING OF THE JEWS (Matthew 27:37).

> And the inscription of His accusation was written above: THE KING OF THE JEWS (Mark 15:26).

> And an inscription also was written over Him in letters of Greek, Latin, and Hebrew: THIS IS THE KING OF THE JEWS (Luke 23:38).

> Now Pilate wrote a title and put it on the cross. And the writing was: JESUS OF NAZARETH, THE KING OF THE JEWS (John 19:19).

There is no reason to suppose that all four of these verses can't be true concerning the inscriptions on the Cross. John (John 19:20) tells us that the charge against Jesus was written in three different languages: Greek, Latin, and Hebrew. Since Matthew's audience was mainly Jewish, he likely quoted the Hebrew inscription (the common language of Palestine): "THIS IS JESUS THE KING OF THE JEWS." Since Luke's audience was mainly the Gentiles, he likely quoted the Greek inscription: "THIS IS THE KING OF THE JEWS."

John mentions that Pilate wrote an inscription (likely someone wrote it at his request), and since Latin was the official language of the Romans, John likely quoted the Latin inscription: "JESUS OF NAZARETH, THE KING OF THE JEWS." Mark could have quoted any of the inscriptions, but merely abbreviated his version to the most relevant portion of the inscription: "THE KING OF THE JEWS."

Although all four inscriptions are slightly different in English, they all contain the statement, "THE KING OF THE JEWS." This was the charge brought by the Jewish leaders against Jesus in the Roman trials (Luke 23:2), and by itself is sufficient to describe Jesus' "crime."

Thus, the content of the four inscriptions is identical, and the minor differences can be attributed to the language of the inscription being quoted by the author, or the author's liberty to quote the part of the sign that he thought was sufficient in his historical account of the events.

An Extra Cainan?

Paul F. Taylor

Does the genealogy in Luke 3:36 give an extra Cainan not found in similar genealogies, such as Genesis 11:12?

There is an alleged error in Luke 3:36. The genealogy gives an extra Cainan not found in similar genealogies, such as Genesis 11:12.

Expositor Dr. John Gill gives ample reasons why this was a copyist error.[31] Gill says:

> This Cainan is not mentioned by Moses in #Ge 11:12 nor has he ever appeared in any Hebrew copy of the Old Testament, nor in the Samaritan version, nor in the Targum; nor is he mentioned by Josephus, nor in #1Ch 1:24 where the genealogy is repeated; nor is it in Beza's most ancient Greek copy of Luke: it indeed stands in the present copies of the Septuagint, but was not originally there; and therefore could not be taken by Luke from thence, but seems to be owing to some early negligent transcriber of Luke's Gospel, and since put into the Septuagint to give it authority: I say "early," because it is in many Greek copies, and in the Vulgate Latin, and all the Oriental versions, even in the Syriac, the oldest of them; but ought not to stand neither in the text, nor in any version: for certain it is, there never was such a Cainan, the son of Arphaxad, for Salah was his son; and with him the next words should be connected.

---

31. Note on Luke 3:36, in: John Gill, D.D., *An Exposition of the Old and New Testament; The Whole Illustrated with Notes, Taken from the Most Ancient Jewish Writings* (London: printed for Mathews and Leigh, 18 Strand, by W. Clowes, Northumberland-Court, 1809). Edited, revised, and updated by Larry Pierce, 1994–1995 for The Word CD-ROM. Available online at http://eword.gospelcom.net/comments/luke/gill/luke3.htm.

Demolishing Contradictions

If the first Cainan was not present in the original, then the Greek may have read in a manner similar to the following. Remember that NT Greek had no spaces, punctuation, or lower case letters.

ΤΟΥΣΑΡΟΥΧΤΟΥΡΑΓΑΥΤΟΥΦΑΛΕΓΤΟΥΕΒΕΡΤΟΥΣΑΛΑ
ΤΟΥΑΡΦΑΞΑΔΤΟΥΣΗΜΤΟΥΝΩΕΤΟΥΛΑΜΕΧ
ΤΟΥΜΑΘΟΥΣΑΛΑΤΟΥΕΝΩΧΤΟΥΙΑΡΕΔΤΟΥΜΑΛΕΛΕΗΛΤ
ΟΥΚΑΙΝΑΝ
ΤΟΥΕΝΩΣΤΟΥΣΗΘΤΟΥΑΛΑΜΤΟΥΘΕΟΥ

If an early copyist glanced at the third line, while copying the first line, it is conceivable that the phrase ΤΟΥΚΑΙΝΑΝ (son of Cainan) may have been copied there.

ΤΟΥΣΑΡΟΥΧΤΟΥΡΑΓΑΥΤΟΥΦΑΛΕΓΤΟΥΕΒΕΡΤΟΥΣΑΛΑΤΟ
ΥΚΑΙΝΑΝ
ΤΟΥΑΡΦΑΞΑΔΤΟΥΣΗΜΤΟΥΝΩΕΤΟΥΛΑΜΕΧ
ΤΟΥΜΑΘΟΥΣΑΛΑΤΟΥΕΝΩΧΤΟΥΙΑΡΕΔΤΟΥΜΑΛΕΛΕΗΛΤ
ΟΥΚΑΙΝΑΝ
ΤΟΥΕΝΩΣΤΟΥΣΗΘΤΟΥΑΛΑΜΤΟΥΘΕΟΥ

There is some circumstantial evidence for this theory. The Septuagint (LXX) is a Greek translation of the Old Testament said to be translated by about 72 rabbis. Early copies of LXX do not have the extra Cainan in Genesis 11, but later copies postdating Luke's gospel do have the extra Cainan.

It might seem odd to suggest that there could be a copyist error in our translations of the Bible. What is even more remarkable to me, however, is that such possible copyist errors are so extremely rare. Paradoxically, the possible existence of such an error merely reinforces how God has preserved His Word through the centuries.

Three Days and Nights

Paul F. Taylor

If Jesus was to be in the grave three days and nights, how do we fit those between Good Friday and Easter Sunday?

If Jesus was to be in the grave three days and nights, how do we fit those between Good Friday and Easter Sunday?

There are several solutions to this problem. Some have suggested that a special Sabbath might have occurred, so Jesus was actually crucified on a Thursday. However, a solution that seems to me to be more convincing is that Jesus was indeed crucified on a Friday but that the Jewish method of counting days was not the same as ours.

In Esther 4:16, we find Esther exhorting Mordecai to persuade the Jews to fast. "Neither eat nor drink for three days, night or day" (NKJV). This was clearly in preparation for her highly risky attempt to see the king. Yet just two verses later, in Esther 5:1, we read: "Now it happened on the third day that Esther put on her royal robes and stood in the inner court of the king's palace." If three days and nights were counted in the same way as we count them today, then Esther could not have seen the king until the fourth day. This is completely analogous to the situation with Jesus' crucifixion and Resurrection.

> For as Jonah was three days and three nights in the belly of the great fish, so will the Son of Man be three days and three nights in the heart of the earth (Matthew 12:40).

> Now after the Sabbath, as the first day of the week began to dawn, Mary Magdalene and the other Mary came to see the tomb (Matthew 28:1).

Then, as they were afraid and bowed their faces to the earth, they said to them, "Why do you seek the living among the dead? He is not here, but is risen! Remember how He spoke to you when He was still in Galilee, saying, 'The Son of Man must be delivered into the hands of sinful men, and be crucified, and the third day rise again' " (Luke 24:5–7).

If the three days and nights were counted the way we count them, then Jesus would have to rise on the fourth day. But by comparing these passages, we can see that in the minds of people in Bible times, "the third day" *is equivalent to* "after three days." In fact, the way they counted was this: part of a day would be counted as one day. The following table, reproduced from the Christian Apologetics and Research Ministry (CARM) website, shows how the counting works.[32]

Day One		Day Two		Day Three	
FRI starts at sundown on Thursday	FRI ends at sundown	SAT starts at sundown on Friday	SAT ends at sundown	SUN starts at sundown on Saturday	SUN ends at sundown
Night	Day	Night	Day	Night	Day
Crucifixion		Sabbath		Resurrection	

This table indicates that Jesus died on Good Friday; that was day one. In total, day one includes the day and the previous night, even though Jesus died in the day. So although only part of Friday was left, that was the first day and night to be counted. Saturday was day two. Jesus rose in the morning of the Sunday. That was day three. Thus, by Jewish counting, we have three days and nights, yet Jesus rose on the third day. It should not be a surprise to us that a different culture used a different method of counting days. As soon as we adopt this method of counting, all the supposed biblical problems with counting the days disappear.

---

32. Matthew Slick, Christian Apologetics and Research Ministry website, "How Long Was Jesus Dead in the Tomb?" http://www.carm.org/diff/Matt12_40.htm.

Acts – Revelation

A Righteous Lie?

Bodie Hodge

Why was Rahab praised for lying in James 2:25 when lying is forbidden in the Ten Commandments?

The context of this is Joshua 2:1–16, when the Israelites were spying out the land that the Lord has promised them. Rahab gave refuge to the spies, hid them, and sent their pursuers off in another direction while directing the Israelites elsewhere. During her discourse with the pursuers, she lied about where the men were. The passage reads:

> Now Joshua the son of Nun sent out two men from Acacia Grove to spy secretly, saying, "Go, view the land, especially Jericho." So they went, and came to the house of a harlot named Rahab, and lodged there (Joshua 2:1).

After she hid the spies, she sent them off:

> And she said to them, "Get to the mountain, lest the pursuers meet you. Hide there three days, until the pursuers have returned. Afterward you may go your way" (Joshua 2:16).

This was a different direction from where she sent the spies' pursuers. This is where the relevant passage in James 2 becomes important:

> Likewise, was not Rahab the harlot also justified by works when she received the messengers and sent them out another way? (James 2:25).

The first thing that needs to be pointed out is that nowhere in this verse is any inclination of Rahab being praised for lying about the spies. Also in Hebrews 11:31, Rahab's faith was praised for receiving the spies in peace. But again, there was no praise for lying. Rahab was not righteous for lying but for her other deeds:

- giving lodging to the spies

- sending the spies in a safe direction

These were the things James considered her righteous for. So, God, who inspired James to write this, never said Rahab's lie was just — only her other actions.

Lying is a breach of the Ninth Commandment and is never condoned by God, regardless of who does the lying or what the circumstances might be. There is no such thing as a "righteous lie." Nonetheless, Rahab acted with integrity based on the limited understanding she had of the God of the Bible at the time. There is evidence here of a changed heart and a changed life. A former prostitute who was once a child of Canaan has become a daughter of Zion.

The most remarkable aspect of this whole story is that Rahab, a Gentile and a common harlot, marries into the family line of David the king, giving birth to Boaz, the husband of Ruth, and becomes showcased as a mother in Israel. What a picture of the incredible humility of our God, whereby the writer to the Hebrews reminds us, "He is not ashamed to call them brethren" (Hebrews 2:11).

How Did Judas Die?

Dr. Georgia Purdom

Did Judas Iscariot die by hanging (Matthew 27:5) or did he die by falling and bursting open (Acts 1:18)?

The relevant passages are:

> Then he threw down the pieces of silver in the temple and departed, and went and hanged himself (Matthew 27:5).

> Now this man purchased a field with the wages of iniquity; and falling headlong he burst open in the middle and all his entrails gushed out (Acts 1:18).

Some people have wrongly assumed that Matthew and Luke (the author of Acts) are contradictory in their account of Judas's death. Since the Bible is inerrant, Judas cannot have died by hanging and died by falling and bursting open. Rather, they are two different viewpoints of the same event. For example, if I saw a car hit a pedestrian, I might simply say that the pedestrian died because he was hit by the car. The coroner who came on the scene later but did not actually see the accident might give a graphic description of the injuries to the pedestrian. Both the coroner and I are describing the same event, just different aspects of it.

Matthew tells us that Judas died by hanging (death is inferred from the passage). Luke, being a doctor, gives us a graphic description of what occurred following the hanging. The reason for ordering the events as such is twofold. First, if someone has fallen and his or her internal organs spilled out, he or she would die and so could not subsequently die from hanging. Second, even when people suffer bad falls, they do not usually burst open and have their internal organs spill out. The skin is very tough, and even when cut in the abdominal area, their internals do not usually spill out. Thus, it is unlikely that Judas could die in this manner merely from falling.

Demolishing Contradictions

Gruesome as it is, Judas's dead body hung in the hot sun of Jerusalem, and the bacteria inside his body would have been actively breaking down tissues and cells. A byproduct of bacterial metabolism is often gas. The pressure created by the gas forces fluid out of the cells and tissues and into the body cavities. The body becomes bloated as a result. In addition, tissue decomposition occurs, compromising the integrity of the skin. Judas's body was similar to an overinflated balloon, and as he hit the ground (due to the branch he hung on or the rope itself breaking) the skin easily broke and he burst open, with his internal organs spilling out.

There is no contradiction surrounding Judas's death; rather, merely two descriptions given by two different authors of the same event.

The Unforgivable Sin

Bodie Hodge

Can all sins be forgiven (Acts 13:39; Titus 2:14; 1 John 1:9) or not (Matthew 12:31; Mark 3:29; Luke 12:10)?

Let's first look at the relevant passages:

and by Him everyone who believes is justified from all things from which you could not be justified by the law of Moses (Acts 13:39).

who gave Himself for us, that He might redeem us from every lawless deed and purify for Himself His own special people, zealous for good works (Titus 2:14).

If we confess our sins, He is faithful and just to forgive us our sins and to cleanse us from all unrighteousness (1 John 1:9).

Therefore I say to you, every sin and blasphemy will be forgiven men, but the blasphemy against the Spirit will not be forgiven men (Matthew 12:31).

but he who blasphemes against the Holy Spirit never has forgiveness, but is subject to eternal condemnation (Mark 3:29).

And anyone who speaks a word against the Son of Man, it will be forgiven him; but to him who blasphemes against the Holy Spirit, it will not be forgiven (Luke 12:10).

There is an important aspect of this alleged contradiction that needs to be discussed to clarify this "problem." First, let's focus on the last three verses above that discuss blasphemy against the Holy Spirit.

The Unforgivable Sin

These passages reveal that there is one sin that is still unforgivable. If God repeats this three times in His Word, then it is important! Is this referring to using the Holy Spirit's name in vain? No, though I wouldn't recommend that either (Exodus 20:7)! What is "blaspheming against the Holy Spirit" then? Is it something more than words?

When one receives Christ, one receives the gift of the Holy Spirit. If one doesn't receive Christ, then one does not receive the Holy Spirit, which is blaspheming against the Holy Spirit. This aligns perfectly with Jesus being the only way and the only name by which one can be saved (John 14:6; cf. Acts 4:12).

The position of the unforgivable sin being rejection of Christ upon death is complementary to the position that it was referring to the statements of the Pharisees challenging Jesus by claiming the Spirit's work was that of Beelzebub's. These are not mutually exclusive.

The greater context of Matthew 12:22–45 (also Mark 3:29 and Luke 12:10) [discussing spirit removal and their potential return], reveals that when Jesus cast out an evil spirit, the Pharisees accused Jesus of doing it by Beelzebub, of which they meant that it was "not by the Spirit of God." Take note that Jesus said this specific blasphemy would not be forgiven "in this age or the age to come" (vs. 32), but also later revealed they will "give an account on the day of judgment for their careless words" (vs. 36–37).

On the flipside, Acts 13:39, Titus 2:14, 1 John 1:9, etc., reveal that believers are justified from "all things," from "every lawless deed," cleansed from "all unrighteousness," etc. Consider 1 John 1:7: "But if we walk in the light as He is in the light, we have fellowship with one another, and the blood of Jesus Christ His Son cleanses us from all sin."

The only way both of these sets of Scriptures can be true is if people who utter such blasphemies (e.g., like the ones the Pharisees uttered) do not become believers. So to the astute reader, Jesus basically revealed that the Pharisees in question would never become believers.

This sin of blasphemy for both the Pharisees as well as others who do not repent and get saved cannot be forgiven, unlike the other sins. If one dies without receiving Christ's forgiveness, then one dies without the Holy Spirit. Hence, one dies without God and without salvation. Often people want to blame God for this, but from a big picture, God is merely giving people what they ask for. If they want life without God, God grants them their bidding in the same way the free gift of eternal life is given through Jesus Christ for those in Him.

But for those not saved, the punishment for the sin of blasphemy against the Holy Spirit must be served. And how long is this? Consider that God is infinite. The punishment from an infinite God is an infinite punishment. This is why we needed a perfect, infinite sacrifice to cover our sin and its repercussions. Jesus Christ, the Son of God, the Creator God (John 1; Colossians 1; Hebrews 1), who is infinite, could take that punishment. But if one rejects Christ and does not receive Him as one's Savior, then that person, whether he or she realizes it or not, will still be punished for sin of blasphemy against the Holy Spirit.

Sadly, many do not realize that the punishment for even one sin is death (Genesis 2:17), which results in an eternal, infinite punishment. And Jesus said:

> And these will go away into everlasting punishment, but the righteous into eternal life (Matthew 25:46).

Now, with this in mind, let's evaluate the other passages and see if this is really in contradiction.

The Subject

First, a question: who is being spoken to in Acts 13:39, Titus 2:14, and 1 John 1:9?

If one pays careful attention, the alleged discrepancy disappears. So who is being spoken to? It is believers in Christ.

This is evidenced by the phrases "everyone who believes," "us," and "we," respectively. With "us" and "we," Paul and John include themselves with their fellow believers.

Believers in Christ have been forgiven all sins and the punishment paid by Christ because of their repentance and belief that

Christ has been saved. And hence, they received the gift of the Holy Spirit and would not be in a position of blaspheming against the Holy Spirit.

Thus, these verses are not in contradiction, as the people being spoken of in Acts 13:39, Titus 2:14, 1 John 1:9 are those who have been forgiven and no longer capable of blasphemy against the Holy Spirit. And those being spoken of in Matthew 12:31, Mark 3:29, and Luke 12:10 are non-believers upon their deaths — when they no longer have the opportunity to receive Christ and receive forgiveness and to turn from their blasphemy against the Holy Spirit.

In laymen's terms, these two sets of verses are speaking about two different sets of people: believers and non-believers. Believers are forgiven all sins, but non-believers will have to deal with at least one big sin — that has eternal consequences.

A special note to readers: please continually pray for those who have not received Christ.

The Firstborn Creator?

Bodie Hodge

How could Jesus be the Creator (John 1:1–3) if He was the firstborn of all creation (Colossians 1:15)?

Christ being the creator should be nothing new or surprising. Some important texts pertinent to this are:

> In the beginning was the Word, and the Word was with God, and the Word was God. He was in the beginning with God. All things were made through Him, and without Him nothing was made that was made (John 1:1–3).

> He is the image of the invisible God, the firstborn over all creation. For by Him all things were created that are in heaven and that are on earth, visible and invisible, whether thrones or dominions or principalities or powers. All things were created through Him and for Him (Colossians 1:15–16).

> "Yet I have set My King on My holy hill of Zion. I will declare the decree: The Lord has said to Me, 'You are My Son, today I have begotten You' " (Psalm 2:6–7).

> For to which of the angels did He ever say: "You are My Son, today I have begotten You"? And again: "I will be to Him a Father, and He shall be to Me a Son"? But when He again brings the firstborn into the world, He says: "Let all the angels of God worship Him" (Hebrews 1:5–6).

Off the cuff, the first thing that needs to be established is that Christ is the Creator God as these passages reveal. Otherwise, Christ would have been the *uncreated creator of the resultant created being*, which is obviously illogical!

Demolishing Contradictions

The alleged contradiction results from an improper understanding of the phrase "firstborn over all of creation" and the meaning and date of the "begetting." Do these really mean the "first created entity" at a time near creation, which some claim is implied here? Absolutely not. A Christian apologist has even pointed out that there is a Greek word for "first created," and it was not used in this instance.[33]

The context of the Psalms and Hebrews passages is clearly of the time of Jesus' ministry on earth, indicating His incarnation some 2,000 years ago, not the beginning or not an alleged beginning to His actual existence. Consider this passage:

> I have found My servant David; with My holy oil I have anointed him. . . . Also I will make him My firstborn, the highest of the kings of the earth (Psalm 89:20–27).

Take notice how David has been allotted the position of firstborn! However, David was the *youngest* — and not the firstborn — of Jesse, his father; the firstborn was Eliab, as indicated in 1 Samuel 17:13. Take notice in Psalm 89:27 how God *assigns* this *title.* Consider also Ephraim's inheritance of the title of firstborn (Jeremiah 31:9), even though he was the younger (Genesis 41:51–52).

Like David and Ephraim, Jesus also received this title. David and Ephraim were obviously not the first created entities, and so it would be illogical to make the claim that Jesus was created due merely to the endowment of this title. Hence, there is no contradiction. Jesus is both the Creator and the One who inherited this elite title.

---

33. Matthew Slick, Col. 1:15, "firstborn of all creation," Christian Apologetics & Research Ministry website, http://www.carm.org/religious-movements/jehovahs-witnesses/col-1 15-firstborn-all-creation.

Accounts Payable

Roger Patterson

Can man be held accountable for his sinful actions, and yet have Christ act as a substitute for his sins?

Relevant passages:

> Surely for your lifeblood I will demand a reckoning; from the hand of every beast I will require it, and from the hand of man. From the hand of every man's brother I will require the life of man. Whoever sheds man's blood, by man his blood shall be shed; for in the image of God He made man (Genesis 9:5–6).

> [Jesus Christ] then would have had to suffer often since the foundation of the world; but now, once at the end of the ages, He has appeared to put away sin by the sacrifice of Himself. And as it is appointed for men to die once, but after this the judgment, so Christ was offered once to bear the sins of many (Hebrews 9:26–28).

> Now all things are of God, who has reconciled us to Himself through Jesus Christ, and has given us the ministry of reconciliation, that is, that God was in Christ reconciling the world to Himself, not imputing their trespasses to them, and has committed to us the word of reconciliation (2 Corinthians 5:18–19).

In Genesis 9:5–6, we read that each man will be held responsible for his actions if he kills another human. It is also clear in Scripture that sin will not be held against those who repent of their sin and trust in Christ's redemptive work on the Cross. It has been asked how men can be held accountable for their own sins, as murder is, and yet Christ can act as a substitute to remove the consequences of sin. The answer comes as we examine the context.

Demolishing Contradictions

As God is making His covenant with Noah and his descendants in Genesis 9, the institution of capital punishment is given. Man has inherent worth because he is made in the image of God. The civil law given to the Israelites and other passages of Scripture make it clear that each person is accountable for his own actions and their consequences. God sets up the temporal punishments that accompany the violation of these civil laws. Civil authority is given to punish those who break the laws. In the case of Genesis 9, the authority is being given to mankind to execute capital punishment. This is a temporal consequence for a temporal action. We can place this in the category of civil justice.

The murder of another human is not only an offense against man, but also an offense against God. When King David had sinned by having Uriah killed and committing adultery with Bathsheba, he recognized his sin against God:

> Wash me thoroughly from my iniquity, and cleanse me from my sin. For I acknowledge my transgressions, and my sin is always before me. Against You, You only, have I sinned, and done this evil in Your sight (Psalm 51:2–4).

Although there was a temporal sin, David recognized that all sins are ultimately an offense against a holy God. In Psalm 7:11 we read that "God is a just judge, and God is angry with the wicked every day."

If a man were to commit murder in our society, he would be violating two laws: the civil law of the government and the holy Law of God (Exodus 20:13). For the act of murder the civil authorities will execute justice through the courts, and the penalty may include capital punishment.

For violating the Law of God, the consequence is much harsher, since the authority is higher. God's eternal justice demands the penalty of eternal death in hell. Because everyone has sinned against a perfectly holy God (Romans 3:23), every person deserves that just punishment.

However, Jesus Christ died on the Cross, and God's wrath against sin was poured out on Him. Those who will repent and put their trust in Christ's substitutionary sacrifice on the Cross can avoid that judgment and spend an eternity in heaven with God (John 3:16–18). The righteousness of Christ and His sacrifice are imputed to us (credited to our account, though we don't deserve it), and God's justice is satisfied (2 Corinthians 5:20–21). There will still be consequences for all who break the civil laws, but those who are in Christ have no fear of the final judgment (1 John 4:17–18).

Conclusion

Bodie Hodge

When it comes to alleged Bible contradictions, skeptics are often quick to point out that the Bible seems full of them. But a closer look at these alleged contradictions reveals the opposite: the Bible is not full of contradictions. After years of studying alleged Bible contradictions, I am convinced that God would not make such remedial mistakes. I once heard that "the Bible is an anvil that has worn out many hammers"; and when attacks on the Bible are in the form of alleged Bible contradictions, it is like taking a plastic fork to a steel anvil! The Bible will stand firm.

But I suggest that many non-Christians want the Bible to be full of contradictions so that it gives them a form of justification for rejecting God. In short, they don't want God to be God, so they don't have to be accountable to Him, but instead they would rather rule their own lives — that is, view themselves as "a god" (Exodus 20:3).

However, many non-Christians may not fully understand the God of the Bible. When mankind sinned against God in Genesis 3 and turned away from Him in the Garden of Eden, the Lord came to seek after them (Genesis 3:8–9) and revealed that there is a plan for salvation from sin (Genesis 3:15). When mankind became so wicked before the Flood (Genesis 6:5), God sought after them through Noah (2 Peter 2:5) and offered a way out of the coming destruction (an ark). When mankind continued in rebellion and sin, God loved us so much to come after us by sending His own Son, Jesus Christ into the creation to save us for all eternity to die the death we all deserve going back to Genesis 3. The Bible says:

> "No one has ascended to heaven but He who came down from heaven, that is, the Son of Man who is in heaven. And as Moses lifted up the serpent in the wilderness, even so must

the Son of Man be lifted up, that whoever believes in Him should not perish but have eternal life. For God so loved the world that He gave His only begotten Son, that whoever believes in Him should not perish but have everlasting life. For God did not send His Son into the world to condemn the world, but that the world through Him might be saved. He who believes in Him is not condemned; but he who does not believe is condemned already, because he has not believed in the name of the only begotten Son of God. And this is the condemnation, that the light has come into the world, and men loved darkness rather than light, because their deeds were evil" (John 3:13–19).

The sad part is that all men love "darkness" rather than "light." This metaphor illustrates that people prefer sin and evil as opposed to forgiveness and salvation. Therefore, many do not receive this free gift of salvation that Christ has offered, and in trying to justify themselves, they try to attack God and His Word with alleged contradictions to try to make God look like an "ogre." But God is not an "ogre," and His Word does not contain any legitimate contradictions.

This short book should be a good introduction to the subject and a good reminder that when it comes to "claims" about a Bible contradiction, the first place to look is the pages of the Bible to see what this claim is all about from God's perspective. As we've seen, such allegations seem to "evaporate into thin air" when one looks at the text logically, in context, and so on.

We want to encourage our readers to stand firm on the authority of the Bible from the very first verse. The God of the Bible created everything (Genesis 1:1–2:4), knows everything (Colossians 2:3), has always been there (Isaiah 46:10), and cannot lie (Titus 1:2). It would be willful rebellion not to trust Him when He speaks on any subject. And God will not contradict Himself when He does speak.

Consider that the Bible stands solidly when faced with alleged Bible contradictions, and then logically it stands solidly in its pronouncement of the Gospel.

Dear reader, if you have not considered the claims of Christ up to this point, I want to encourage you to do that now and meditate of what the Lord has done for you.

I would urge you to be reconciled to God, and suggest you speak freely to an offended God in prayer at this point and tell Him that you realize that you are a sinner (we all are according to Romans 5:12) and have fallen short of a perfect God (we have all fallen short according to Romans 3:23). Tell God that you repent of your sins (turn from your sin and be sincerely sorry for those actions) and ask God to forgive you of your sins (Acts 3:19 and 17:20). Now, this doesn't make you perfect from now on, just forgiven — after all, no Christian is perfect, but we strive to be better every day because we want to love and obey God in return (1 Corinthians 15:34). Then ask Christ, the Son of God, to come into your life, and dedicate yourself to Him and believe in Him and receive the free gift of salvation.

> "Sirs, what must I do to be saved?" So they said, "Believe on the Lord Jesus Christ, and you will be saved" (Acts 16:30–31).

If you prayed to receive the Lord, I want to welcome you to the family and encourage you to find a Bible-believing church in your area where you can find fellowship with other Christians and grow to know more about God, the Bible, and living a life that is God-honoring.

Appendix : Regarding a Righteous Lie

Bodie Hodge

(Answering a couple of questions about the alleged contradiction entitled: Why was Rahab praised for lying in James 2:25 when lying is forbidden in the Ten Commandments?)

Question 1: You, know I almost hate to do this because I know how much e-mail you guys handle. . . . But I want to respond to Bodie Hodge's "contradictions" article on Rahab's "lie." Bodie is almost always right on the mark and is probably my favorite feedback man, but in this case I have to take exception to his saying that it is always wrong to lie. . . . The ninth commandment says we should never bear false witness against our neighbor (or anyone). But if the Nazis are looking for Jews, and you know where they are, it would not be wrong to lie, in order to protect them, nor would this be bearing false witness "against" someone. . . . I think in the same way the Israeli midwives lied to the Egyptians about the birthing of male babies in Moses's day. . . . I know it's a rare exception, but there may be other circumstances when it might be appropriate to "lie," although obviously, 99 percent of the time it would be wrong. . . . Keep up the good work, all of you, your ministry is the most awesome in the world, just blows me away.   — M.H.

Thank you for contacting Answers in Genesis and thanks for the comments. I know this can be a touchy subject, but please bear with me as I try to explain. Keep in mind that I, too, am not perfect but will try to answer as scripturally as possible. (Also, sorry for the length — but this will allow me the breadth that I did not have with the contradiction article on Rahab.)

Righteous Lies?

Bearing false witness is a lie, and in Hebrew the word for *false* in Exodus 20:16 is *sheqer,* which literally means "lie." It is derived from the Hebrew word *shaqar,* which means "deal falsely, be false, trick, and cheat." There are many verses in the Bible that reaffirm the Ninth Commandment, and a couple are:

> You shall not steal, nor deal falsely, nor lie to one another (Leviticus 19:11).

> I have not written to you because you do not know the truth, but because you know it, and that no lie is of the truth (1 John 2:21).

The devil is the father of lies (John 8:44), and one lie to God the Holy Spirit was worthy of instant death for Ananias (Acts 5:3–5). Paul points out that even if he were to lie for the glory of God, he would be deemed a sinner for such an act:

> For if the truth of God has increased through my lie to His glory, why am I also still judged as a sinner? (Romans 3:7).

In light of such passages, does a "righteous lie" really exist? The most common example sent to me was envisioning the Holocaust and being placed in the position of lying to potentially protect someone's life. Like most, if placed in such a difficult situation, it would be very difficult. In fact, I could never be sure what I would do, especially if it were a loved one.

But consider for a moment that we are all already sentenced to die because we are sinners (Romans 5:12). It is going to happen regardless. If a lie helps keep someone alive for a matter of moments compared to eternity, was the lie, which is high treason against the Creator, worth it? It would be like sitting in a cell on death row and when the guards come to take your roommate to the electric chair, you lie to the guards and say you don't know where the person went — while your roommate is hiding under his covers on the bed.

Does it really help? Since we are all sinners (Romans 3:23), death is coming for us, and there is an appointed time (Ecclesiastes 3:2).

> The truthful lip shall be established forever, but a lying tongue is but for a moment (Proverbs 12:19).

Is it worth sinning against God to try to buy a moment of time next to eternity? Intentionally lying is foolish and would only harm the extent of your own life (Ecclesiastes 7:17). Let's look further at Scripture for an example of a situation where a lie could have saved a life.

Stephen

In Acts 6–7, Stephen preached Christ, and men came against him. This culminated with a question by the high priest in Acts 7:1 who said, "Are these things so?"

At this point, Stephen could have done a "righteous lie" to save his life so that he could have many more years to preach the gospel. However, Stephen laid a long and appropriate foundation for Christ — then preached Christ. And they killed him.

But this event triggered a persecution that sent the gospel to the Gentiles (Acts 11:19) and peaked with Paul (who consented to Stephen's death) coming to Christ and taking the message to the Gentiles and writing several books of the New Testament. The Lord had a greater purpose for Stephen — even though it cost him his life. Keep in mind, however, that this, and other examples, are about the person in question — not another.

Do We Know What God Had in Mind?

I often wonder if a Nazi soldier asked if someone was there hiding and they told the truth before God, could the Lord have in mind a greater purpose? Could God have used that person to free a great many people who ultimately died in the Holocaust? Or have done something to stop the war earlier? Or cause a great number of Jews and Nazis to come to know Christ? It is possible, but we simply cannot know. And one should not dwell too long on "what ifs" anyway.

No doubt, there is great value in the truth (John 8:32). As fallible, sinful human beings, our imperfect thoughts may not be able to comprehend what God has in mind, and we need to strive to trust God when He speaks on this subject, regardless how hard it may be. We need to place our faith fully in Christ and trust in God in all things — and not lean on our own understanding (Proverbs 3:5).

I'm not saying this to be "preachy," because I really don't know what I would do in such a situation. However, I would pray that the Lord would grant me the wisdom to know what to say and how to say it — but more preferably — how to avoid being in that situation in the first place.

If Forced into This Situation . . . What Then?

Let's consider again the Nazi-Holocaust situation. There seems to be a conflict in the situation to lie before God to try to save someone else's life.[34] The result is often called the "greater good" or "lesser of two evils."

I've been told in the past that the lesser of these two evils would be to lie to save a life — hence the common phrase "a righteous lie." This is often justified by appealing to the command to love our neighbor (Romans 13:9).

But how does God view this, remembering that God is a discerner of our motives? To God, a lie for selfish motive was worthy of death to Ananias. But in fact, just one sin is worthy of death (Genesis 2:17). (This should be a reminder that we should continually praise God for His grace that is bestowed upon us.) But let's look at Scripture again. The two greatest commandments are:

> Then one of the scribes came, and having heard them reasoning together, perceiving that He had answered them well, asked Him, "Which is the first commandment of all?"

---

34. In reality, it more like lying to keep them from going to a work camp — at least that is what most thought anyway. Few lay people within the Nazi empire were aware of what was going on behind the scenes at some camps, particularly the six death camps. Most knew they were working in slave-like conditions in work camps or concentration camps though — they could only speculate on the extent of what was going on.

> Jesus answered him, "The first of all the commandments is: 'Hear, O Israel, the LORD our God, the LORD is one. And you shall love the LORD your God with all your heart, with all your soul, with all your mind, and with all your strength.' This is the first commandment. And the second, like it, is this: 'You shall love your neighbor as yourself.' There is no other commandment greater than these" (Mark 12:28–31).

Jesus tells us that all the commandments can be summed up into these two statements. But of these two, the first is to love the Lord your God with all your heart, with all your soul, with all your mind, and with all your strength. So, this would trump the second. Our actions toward God should trump our actions toward men. Peter also affirmed this:

> But Peter and the other apostles answered and said: "We ought to obey God rather than men" (Acts 5:29).

If we love God, we should obey Him (John 14:15). To love God first means to obey Him first — before looking at our neighbor. So is the "greater good" trusting God when He says not to lie or trusting in our fallible, sinful minds about the uncertain future?

Consider this carefully. In the situation of a Nazi beating on the door, we have assumed a lie would save a life, but really we don't know. So one would be opting to lie and disobey God *without* the certainty of saving a life — keeping in mind that all are ultimately condemned to die physically.[35] Besides, whether one lied or not may not have stopped the Nazi soldiers from searching the house anyway.

As Christians, we need to keep in mind that Jesus Christ reigns. All authority has been given to Him (Matthew 28:18), and He sits on the throne of God at the right hand of the Father (Acts 2:33; Hebrews 8:1). Nothing can happen without His say. Even Satan could not touch Peter without Christ's approval (Luke 22:31). Regardless if one were to lie or not, Jesus Christ is in control of

---

35. This does not mean that atrocities such as genocide are acceptable. These atrocities should be opposed as well, in keeping with the Word of God.

timing every person's life and able to discern our motives. It is not for us to worry over what might happen, but rather to place our faith and obedience in Christ and to let Him do the reigning. For we do not know the future, whereas God has been telling the end from the beginning (Isaiah 46:10).

> Question 2: Wow, you put a lot of work into that answer, Bodie, and from a biblical basis, too. I agree with you 100 percent about lying to protect yourself, that could be interpreted as mere cowardice, and I think most of your biblical examples dealt with that. However there is a Scripture in Exodus 1:15–22, in which the Jewish midwives are told to kill all the male babies they delivered but refused to do so. When asked why they hadn't destroyed the babies, they told the Egyptians the Hebrew women simply gave birth faster than the Egyptian women, and had the babies before the midwives got there. Verse 17, however, says that the Jewish midwives saved the male children alive, so here they are lying not only to save the male babies but probably to escape punishment from the Egyptians. Verse 20 says that God dealt well with the midwives for doing this. I think this is one of the rare examples or cases where lying would truly not be offensive to our Creator. At any rate, I think this Scripture shows that not all lies are equal, at least to my mind. In that most lies are done for self advancement, self protection, greed, etc., but some are done at least with the intention of protecting others, their reputations or physical selves. I can't fault your stance, though, your conscience and the Word must be your guide. Keep up the good work.   —M.H.

I looked up the passage about the midwives, and I, personally, don't believe they lied. Scripture doesn't really say they did. Please see the context:

> Then the king of Egypt spoke to the Hebrew midwives, of whom the name of one was Shiphrah and the name of the other Puah; and he said, "When you do the duties of a midwife for the Hebrew women, and see them on the birthstools,

if it is a son, then you shall kill him; but if it is a daughter, then she shall live." But the midwives feared God, and did not do as the king of Egypt commanded them, but saved the male children alive. So the king of Egypt called for the midwives and said to them, "Why have you done this thing, and saved the male children alive?" And the midwives said to Pharaoh, "Because the Hebrew women are not like the Egyptian women; for they are lively and give birth before the midwives come to them."

Therefore God dealt well with the midwives, and the people multiplied and grew very mighty. And so it was, because the midwives feared God, that He provided households for them.

So Pharaoh commanded all his people, saying, "Every son who is born you shall cast into the river, and every daughter you shall save alive" (Exodus 1:15–22).

Naturally, their fear of God led them to refuse the order to murder. It makes more sense to me that they could have informed the Hebrew wives what the pharaoh had commanded, and thus, many of the Israelite women were giving birth *before* the midwives would arrive so they would not be in a position of killing the child. Perhaps the midwives took their time to arrive as well. That would allow the children to survive and the midwives to speak the truth to pharaoh.

What would make pregnant mothers more vigorous or lively to have the child born? Make them aware that if they do not give birth quickly their child's life may be in danger. There are any number of ways the mothers and midwives could have avoided a lie.

Too Many Questions for Just One Book

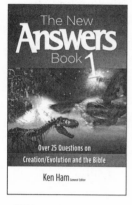

ISBN: 978-0-89051-509-9

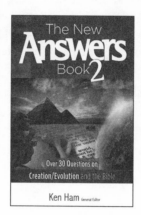

ISBN: 978-0-89051-537-2

ISBN: 978-0-89051-579-2

Christians live in a culture with more questions than ever — questions that affect one's acceptance of the Bible as authoritative and trustworthy. Now, discover easy-to-understand answers that teach core truths of the Christian faith and apply the biblical worldview to subjects like evolution, the fall of Lucifer, Noah and the Flood, the star of Bethlehem, dinosaurs, death and suffering, and much more.

Explore these and other topics, answered biblically and logically in these three books from the world's largest apologetics ministry, Answers in Genesis.

Timely and scientifically solid, *The New Answers Books 1, 2*, and *3* offer concise answers from leading creationist Ken Ham and scientists such as Dr. David Menton, Dr. Georgia Purdom, Dr. Andrew Snelling, Dr. Jason Lisle, Dr. Elizabeth Mitchell, and many more.

6 x 9 • Paperback • 384 pages • $14.99 each

Available at your local Christian bookstore or at www.nlpg.com

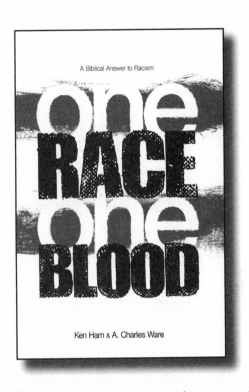

A Biblical Answer to Racism

one
RACE
one
BLOOD

Ken Ham & A. Charles Ware

Many people do not realize how intimately connected the theory of evolution and the worst racist ideology in history are. Join Answers in Genesis president Ken Ham and president of Crossroads Bible College Dr. Charles Ware as they examine the racist historical roots of evolutionary thought and what the Bible has to say about this disturbing issue.

This fascinating book gives a thorough history of the effect of evolution on the history of the United States, including slavery and the civil rights movement, and goes beyond to show the global harvest of death and tragedy that stems from Darwin's controversial theories. You will also learn what the Christian's view of racism should be and what the Bible has to say about it in a compassionate and uniquely compelling perspective.

ISBN: 978-0-89051-601-0 • 6 x 9 • Paperback • 208 pages • $13.99 each

Available at your local Christian bookstore or at www.nlpg.com

Join the
Conversation

Ask the experts

Build relationships

Share your thoughts

Download free resources

Creation
Conversations
.com

This is your invitation to our
online community of believers.